INDIAN POLITICAL THOUGHT

GANDHI TO GODSE

VENKATA MOHAN

Contents

Contents

Contents

Preface

How was the Indian nation conceived out of a diverse society of conflicting castes and religions which was under British occupation? What was its supposed destiny? Why did the country have to be partitioned? Is India on the path its founding fathers envisaged for it? This book invites you to explore such questions and reflect on them.

Uniquely this book brings out the religious heritage of Indian political thought. Ramakrishna Paramahamsa, whom we have on the cover page, can be seen as the manifestation of ancient India's wisdom that appeared at the right time and right place – for enabling the educated Hindus to think of their past in more confident ways.

Hope you enjoy reading.
Venkata Mohan
July 2022

Also By Venkata Mohan

1. Political Thought
2. IR Theory
3. India Among Nations
4.. Modern World: Ideas & Ideals
5. Cultural Anthropology
6. Caste & Religion in India
7. Tribal India & Social Thought
8. Sociological Thought
9. Economy: Concepts & Issues
10. Anthropological Thought
11. Ethical Thought
12. Moksha, Afterlife & Science

Rammohan Roy

CHAPTER ONE

Vedanta as Hinduism

Rammohan Roy (1772–1833) is regarded as a great reformer of Hindu society. He actively cooperated with the British in calling for a change in certain Hindu practices and getting some others banned. He took a particular view of Hinduism by which he could say many social evils associated with Hinduism were not an essential part of it and the Hindu religion included many modern values.

Roy's father was a zamindar. Roy was involved in business, but he was also a scholar. He knew as many as 10 languages – Persian, Arabic, English, Urdu, Hindi, Hebrew, Greek, Latin and French. He knew classical Greek philosophy, Persian and Arabic literature, Vedantic philosophy and modern Western thought. He read much of the world's religious literature – Bible, Quran, Sufism, Buddhism, Vedas and Upanishads. And he also read Western political works – Plato, Aristotle, Locke, Hume, and Bentham.

Rammohan Roy had great knowledge, but his focus was on Hinduism. He was trying to understand what it is. It consists of too many texts, practices, philosophies, and schools of thought. There was Brahminism, superstition and irrationality in it. Hinduism is not one thing, there are so many bad things and many good things.

Rammohan Roy took what he regarded as the highest element in Hinduism, its philosophy of Vedanta, and considered it as its essence. Vedanta is based on the belief that the individual is a manifestation of God. When the individual realises this, it is regarded as liberation. This philosophy was popularised by Adi Shankaracharya in the 8th century.

Rammohan Roy took Vedanta as being central to Hinduism. This was his innovative approach. Vedanta promotes the values that the West glorified, such as rationality and equality, and excludes what Roy thought as the evils of the Indian society.

Rammohan Roy established Brahmoism based on Vedanta. There is one God, he is infinite, manifest everywhere, and he is the single author of the universe. He is called Brahman. The word 'Brahman' needs to be differentiated from a similar-sounding caste name and a similar-sounding god's name. An individual comes from God and finally goes back to God. An individual should follow right conduct, he should use his reason, he should seek knowledge, and he has the free will to alter his life as he chooses.

Rammohan Roy rejects fate. And there need be no rituals, no intermediaries between Brahman and oneself, no priests, nor any specific places to worship. The Brahman is one and formless, so there is no room for idolatry and polytheism. One has to realise the truth through reason and knowledge. There are no prophets, no avatars, and there is nothing like a revelation. Since the Brahman is manifested in every life form, distinctions based on caste, creed, and race are entirely baseless. How about the soul, rebirth and karma? Roy doesn't take any stand on them and leaves those beliefs to the individuals.

Rammohan Roy entirely rules out polytheism, idolatry and such things which he regarded as being the real problems with the Indian tradition. Also, he incorporates Western values in his approach. There are no distinctions based on caste, creed and race. You can't blindly believe a scripture. Scripture should be subjected to reason, and when there is a conflict between scripture and reason, one should go with reason. One cannot say that some sacred text contains the final truth based solely on dogmatic belief.

Rammohan Roy's A Gift to Deists (1803) describes the evils of contemporary Bengali society. The priestly class were held responsible for these evils. Between 1815 and 1823, he published the translations of several Upanishads. Roys' Vedanta as well as Upanishads were based on Shankara's perspective. Roy thought of himself as doing the work that Martin Luther did for Christianity. Martin Luther caused the main split in Christianity and formed Protestantism. It was to propagate his new Vedantic approach that Rammohan Roy founded a society called the Brahmo Sabha in 1828, which later came to be called Brahmo Samaj. Samaj means society, it's a society for the worshipers of Brahman, the ultimate reality.

Rammohan Roy wanted the state to take up religious as well as social reform in the case of the Hindus and introduce Western education in India. Western education would bring science and technology, it would also bring reasoning and questioning to the minds of the people. It would bring modern values to society.

Rammohan Roy's work of promoting Vedanta and social reform was eventually taken up by the likes of Vivekananda, Aurobindo, and even Gandhi. Where is Vedanta in Gandhi's approach? Gandhi's Satyagraha is based on the ability to transform the opponent, which is possible because there is the ultimate reality even in a bad person as much as in a good person.

Roy identified Vedanta as the essence of Hinduism and created a template for scores of gurus and religious leaders in the twentieth century. He was gearing up the Indian society for the project of modernisation and its eventual independence.

Think on it

1. What do you know about Roy's Knowledge?
2. What is Vedanta?
3. What is Brahmoism?
4. How did Roy exclude idolatry and polytheism and include reason, free will and equality in Hinduism?
5. Why was reinterpreting Hinduism important?

Jyotirao Phule

CHAPTER TWO

Brahmins Wrote Vedas to Enslave Natives

Brahmo Samaj, Arya Samaj and Prarthana Samaj – all of them were trying to see modern values in the Indian scriptures. They were trying hard to see only what is good in them. They didn't blame the scriptures for the social evils related to Hinduism, such as the repression of women and the caste system. To blame the scriptures would be to blame Hinduism. To blame Hinduism would be to blame India's past, India's very identity.

However, one man refused to play this game and spoke very boldly. He said the evils could be traced back to the Hindu scriptures. He was Jyotirao Phule (1827-90). This would be the position of Pandita Ramabai and Dr B.R. Ambedkar, but the first person who took this position was Jotirao Phule, whom Ambedkar considered one of his gurus. Phule was arguing on the basis of historical evidence that was just coming to light about the Aryans and where they came from.

Phule was born in Pune in a family from a caste of gardeners called Malis. His father was a contractor. The British created certain new economic activities, including contracting and building, and Phule's father could become a successful contractor. Phule himself would become a successful businessman.

Phule attended the local Scottish Mission High School. On one occasion when he attended a Brahmin friend's wedding, he was insulted very much. Phule and the groom were close friends but the groom's relatives did not like 'an impure person' attending a Brahmin ceremony. Phule was hurt and around that time he happened to read Thomas Paine's Rights of Man, which impacted him.

Phule finished his education in 1848. The same year, along with his wife Savitribai whom he had taught reading and writing, Phule started a school for Shudra and Atishudra girls. As his school was opposed by the upper-caste people of his village, his father asked him to close it or leave home.

Phule left home. And with the support of some people, he started more schools for girls. By 1852, he had 3 schools with 273 girls in all, but they were all closed by 1858 due to lack of funds. The funds got affected because of the 1857 revolt. Phule was engendering so much opposition with his social activities that earlier, in 1856, there was an attempt on his life. However, the British government treated him well and he was a member of the Pune municipal council between 1876 and 1882.

Phule wrote Gulamgiri (Slavery) in 1873. This book became the basis for the organisation he founded in the same year, Satyashodak Samaj. Unlike other organisations at that time, this organisation was founded by a lower-caste person, a Shudra. Phule wrote Shetkari Asud (The Whipcord of the Cultivators) in 1881 about Shudra farmers. He wrote Sarvajanik Satya Dharma Pustak (The Book of the True Faith) around the time of his death in 1890 and it was published the next year.

Slavery

The book Slavery makes use of the Aryan migration theory. "Recent researches have demonstrated beyond a shadow of a doubt that the Brahmins were not the aborigines of India." "The original inhabitants with whom the Brahmins fought were not inappropriately termed Rakshas, that is the protectors of the land. They eventually succeeded in establishing their supremacy and subjugating the aborigines to their entire control. Accounts of these conquests, enveloped with a mass of incredible fiction, are found in the books of the Brahmins."

Phule was saying that the Aryans came, subordinated the natives, and wrote scriptures to keep them down, creating Hinduism in the process. This is indeed a very valid stance. Incidentally, it corroborates Marx's historical materialism, which states that material conditions give rise to other aspects of culture, including religion. Religion was used to dominate people, for material benefits, and to create slaves. Phule, without knowing about Marxism – Marx (1818-83) was Phule's contemporary –was using the theory of historical materialism to explain how Hinduism evolved.

Phule says that the Aryans devised, "that weird system of mythology, the ordination of caste, and the code of cruel and inhuman laws, to which we can find no parallel amongst the other nations." Racial differences gave rise to caste differences and formed the basis of the Hindu social order.

Phule ridiculed the Brahminical narratives. "If Brahma has four faces, he must have had eight breasts, four genitals and four anuses." He wrote, "Parasharam was a bully, vicious and barbarous villain." Phule exalted Bali whom the Brahmin boy Vamana sent to the nether world.

"Brahmins think of cow-piss as sacred. They drink cow piss and purify themselves. And the same bhats and Brahmins think of the shudra farmer as low. How will the farmers and Brahmins unite?" Phule was asking, was cow urine more sacred than a human being? He was not in any way implying that Hinduism got corrupted or distorted over time, Hinduism as such is a dehumanising force. It is being true to Hinduism to believe that cow urine is more sacred than some human beings.

Phule's main concern at that time was the Brahminical colonialism that had been in sway for thousands of years and not the more recent British colonialism. He didn't seek Indian independence, he was more concerned about the plight of large sections of the Indian population consisting of Shudras, currently called OBCs, and Atishudras, currently called Dalits or SCs. The word 'Dalit', meaning the crushed, was introduced by Phule only. He opened a well in his house for the use of people of lower castes, because they were not allowed to use many village wells reserved for the upper-caste people.

It is not that Phule did not see the exploitation of British rule. In Shetkarya Asud, he clearly stated that the peasants' plight worsened during British rule. He knew the British would not stay here forever. "The English are here today, but who knows whether they will be here tomorrow? They won't be there till eternity. Therefore, all the shudras should make haste to free themselves from the ancestral slavery of these bhats." Phule was more concerned about releasing the lower-caste people from the clutches of the upper-caste people.

Phule believed that education was the way to empower the lower castes. "Because the Arya Brahmins have kept them ignorant for their own selfish purposes, the farmers do not have the power of balanced thought." By 'farmers', he was referring to the Shudras. Phule wanted mass education. "The greater portion of the revenue of the India empire are derived from the ryot's labour. That government should expend profusely a large portion of revenue thus raised on the education of the higher classes, for it is these only who take advantage of it, is anything but just or equitable." The higher spending of the government on higher education, which at that time people like Ranade were asking for, was not right. Phule wanted a massive expansion of primary education. Higher education benefits only the elites.

Phule was consulted for the Hunter Commission of 1882, which was the first education commission for modern India. He recommended the expansion of primary education. He wanted more attention to be given to the students from the lower castes, and he said teachers themselves should come from the lower castes.

Phule looked at the gender issue the same way he looked at the caste issue. Women were "victims of Brahminic culture and power in common with other lower caste and untouchable people." Women, Shudras and Atishudras were all victims of the upper castes. This way Hinduism was benefitting very few people. The women were denied education, for the same reason the lower castes were denied.

The Brahmin women were the worst victims. Phule ran a home for pregnant Brahmin widows. There used to be many young widows at that time. Girls used to get married at a very early age, and when they became widows, their presence itself was considered inauspicious. Their heads would be shaved, and their movements would be very restricted. And they were vulnerable to sexual exploitation by their relatives and others. They would get unwanted pregnancies, and when the children were born, the women would not know what to do with them. Phule distributed pamphlets saying, "Widows, come here and deliver your baby safely and secretly. It is up to your discretion whether you want to keep the baby in the centre or take it with you." Nobody had done anything like this. He advocated widow remarriage, and he was against tonsuring the heads of the widows. Phule himself adopted one boy child delivered by a widow.

Hinduism was so deeply exploitative to Phule that he considered the Islamic rulers of the medieval ages to be potential rescuers. In Sarvajanik Satya Dharma Pustak, Phule wrote: "Muslims were sent by God to India to rescue people from caste-based slavery. But they soon immersed themselves in luxury and betrayed God. Then God deprived them of their power, civilised the English primitives, granted them valour and sent them to rescue the shudras and atishudras from the Aryan Brahmins. And some Englishmen were sincerely doing this work."

Phule was not only not against the British rule, he wanted them to be here and civilise us. Phule was quite an exception among the Indian thinkers of that time who were too busy glorifying Hinduism.

Think on it

1. What incident spurred Phule to see the reality of the caste system?
2. What was the chief motive behind the Indian scriptures?
3. According to Phule, why did untouchability exist?
4. What were Phule's views on British rule?
5. What were Phule's ideas on education?
6. What were Phule's ideas on gender injustice?

Syed Ahmad Khan

CHAPTER THREE

Initiating Critical Thinking among Muslims

Syed Ahmad Khan (1817–98) is regarded as a great Islamic reformer from South Asia. He is best known for his contribution to education for Muslims. In 1859, he set up a school at Murdabad and another school at Ghazipur. And in 1863, he set up a scientific society for the Muslims. In 1875, he founded the Muhammadan Anglo-Oriental (MAO) College. This college became Aligarh Muslim University later and was at the forefront of providing education to the Muslims.

Khan was 10 years older than Phule. He entered the service of East India Company in 1838 and retired as a judge in 1876. He served in the Imperial Legislative Council from 1878 to 1880 and the legislative council of North West Province from 1887 to 1893.

On 1857 Revolt

Khan held that there shouldn't be any hostility between the British and the Muslims. He felt that the Muslims, instead of fighting the British, should learn from them certain good things like education. When the 1857 revolt took place, he wrote that it was not because the Muslims had any issues with the British being the rulers but only because they misunderstood the British policies. He said there was a fear that the Christian religion was going to be imposed on them, that foreign customs were going to be forced on them and that missionaries were being financed by the governments. As a solution, he proposed that native people should have participation in the legislative councils so that the government would know their fears and opinions.

Khan wrote the book The Causes of the Indian Mutiny, presenting a critique of the British policies that led to the misunderstanding between the government and the people. The British government liked his assessment. During the mutiny, Khan remained loyal to the British and even saved many officers' families from the revolting soldiers. He was praised for this by the government. Khan wrote The Mahomedan Commentary on the Holy Bible in 1862 to develop a common understanding and bridge the gulf between the Muslims and the British.

Religious views

Syed Ahmad Khan said that a Muslim should have the Quran in one hand and science in another. Can the Quran and Islam really stand the scrutiny of science?

Khan believed in Allah and the prophet. He saw the Quran as God's word. Khan's proposal was one should interpret the Quran in the light of science. He said the word of God and the work of God can't be contradicting each other.

When a colleague pointed to him, 'Look, science keeps changing, does it mean that the Quran should also change?' Khan said, 'Yes, precisely that is my point.' We do not have to go by the literal meaning of the verses. This is close to Rammohan Roy's position that in case of conflict between scripture and reason, one should go by reason.

Khan boldly went against some views sacred to the Muslims. Muslims consider sacred not only the Quran but also the Hadiths. Hadiths are the lore of what Prophet Mohammad said or did, as supposedly recalled by others. Islamic scholars agree that all the

Hadiths cannot be considered reliable. Scholars try to find out which is an authentic Hadith and which is a fake one, but the task is not easy.

As Islam spread, many new Hadiths were being added to the existing ones. Different caliphates had different Hadiths. After reading a large number of Hadiths and looking at all kinds of things attributed to Prophet Mohammed, Khan concluded that most of them are really unreliable. Khan more or less rejected the validity of all the Hadiths.[1] These stories attributed so many miracles to Prophet Mohammed, and Khan dismissed these miracles on the ground that they would not be acceptable to science. He also did not believe in angels and such supernatural elements.

There is one very important belief among the Muslims that the prophet went from Mecca to Jerusalem and from there went flying up to heaven and met Allah and other prophets. This supernatural act is considered proof of the prophethood of Mohammed. Syed Ahmad Khan simply ruled it out saying all of it must have been a dream.

Khan faced much opposition from the orthodox ulemas. Khan believed Islam as such is not irrational but it was the ulemas who made it a dogmatic religion. These views were not only radical for that time but are so even now.

A particular book that made Syed Ahmad Khan take a critical look at Islam was William Muir's The Life of Mohammad, published between 1858 and 1861 in four volumes. The author presented a theory that what inspired the prophet was not God but the devil. This book was very serious criticism of Islam. Muir also criticised many aspects of Islam such as polygamy, divorce, slavery, the veiling of women, intolerance, absence of freedom of thought and personal opinion. He concluded, "The sword of Muhammed and the Quran are the most stubborn enemies of civilisation, liberty and the truth which the world has yet known." At first, this book deeply offended Khan.

Khan published a rebuttal in 1870 in a series of essays. Many of the things that Muir attributed to Islam were taken from the

Hadiths. Even when Khan was defending Islam against Muir's criticism, he did not defend the miracles. But this critical engagement with Muir started changing Khan's views regarding Islam and he grew more sceptical.

Education of women

On the education of women, however, Khan had very regressive views. During the 1860s and 70s, he was favourably disposed to female education, but later he retracted. He maintained the traditional view that the man should be the bread-earner and the woman should be at home. He said that the girls should learn "domestic crafts, respect for their elders, affection for their husband, care of the children and understanding of religious tenets."[2] There is no need for them to learn science.

Khan felt that if a male is educated then it automatically helps the females. "For enlightened fathers, brothers and husbands would naturally be most anxious to educate their female relations." He said, "If boys were educated, the rights of girls would improve." On this issue, he was lagging behind many fellow Muslims. For example, in 1888, the Mohammadan Educational Conference at Lahore, passed a resolution that Muslims should establish schools for the education of Muslim girls. This resolution was opposed by Khan. But it could get passed because of the initiative of Theodore Beck, then principal of MAO college.

Two-nation theory

Syed Ahmad Khan is known as the father of the two-nation theory. Khan used to say that Hindus and Muslims were "two eyes of the beautiful bride that is Hindustan," but over time, he changed his opinion. Some say one factor that contributed to the change was that Khan wanted Urdu as the lingua franca in India and the Hindus wanted Hindi. Because of this Hindi vs Urdu controversy, Khan realised that progressively the Hindus would dominate the political scene.

After the formation of the INC, Khan asked the Muslims not to take part in its activities, because if the INC achieves what it wants to achieve, then it would lead to Hindu domination. What serves the Hindus is different from what serves the Muslims. For positing that the interests of Muslims and Hindus diverge, Khan is regarded as the father of the two-nation theory – Hindus and Muslims as two separate people, two separate nations.

Khan said, "So long as differences of race and creed and the distinctions of caste form an important element in the socio-political life of India, the system of election can't be safely adopted. The larger community would totally override the interests of the smaller community." He wrote this in 1883, and at that time, the Muslim population was 20% of the total.

Khan's assessment that a democracy would lead to majoritarianism may be right, but this statement why the British rule is preferable to Hindu majoritarianism is not in a good taste! "At this time our nation is in a bad state in regards to education and wealth, but God has given us the light of religion and the Quran is present for our guidance, which has ordained them and us to be friends. Now God has made them rulers over us. Therefore we should cultivate friendship with them and should adopt that method by which their rule may remain permanent and firm in India, and may not pass into the hands of the Bengalis. If we join the political movement of the Bengalis our nation will reap a loss, for we do not want to become subjects of the Hindus instead of the People of the Book."[3] The Muslims can be ruled by the Christians, the people of the Book, but not by the Hindus.

Think on it

1. What were Khan's views on the 1857 revolt?
2. How did Khan become closer to the British during the 1857 revolt?

3. What did Khan want from Muslims of India in the colonial setting?
4. According to Khan, should Quran's interpretation be fixed?
5. What were Khan's views on miracles, angels and the Hadiths?
6. What was the nature of Khan's engagement with William Muir's book on Islam?
7. What were Khan's views on the education of Muslim women?

[1] Response of Sayyid Ahmad Khan to Sir William Muir's evaluation of Hadit Literature by Alan M Guenther, JSTOR

[2] Sir Syed Ahmad Khan and Muslim Female Education: A Study in Contradictions by Nasreen Ahmed, JSTOR

[3] Taken from New World Encyclopedia

Pandita Ramabai

CHAPTER FOUR

A Feminist Rejects Hinduism

Pandita Ramabai (1858–1922) was one of the earliest feminists in India. Her life was of a rare kind. She faced many personal struggles and tragedies. She took some bold and unpopular decisions. Reading about her, we might wonder whether a person like her really ever existed.

The childhood of Ramabai was very unusual. As a child in a Brahmin family, she lived the life of a peregrine, going from one place to another with her parents and two older siblings. They used to read or sing scriptures near temples for a living.

Ramabai's father was a Marathi Chitpavan Brahmin. He was a liberal thinker. He wanted to educate his wife but faced opposition from conservative Brahmins. There was a debate on whether a woman could learn Sanskrit and he won the debate, but that did not get him any closer to the people. He decided to move to a forest and start an ashram for boys. There he also educated his wife and his daughter Rama in Sanskrit texts. Rama – 'bai' is a suffix that was added later – became well-versed in many kinds of Sanskrit texts such as dharma sutras and others.

But tragedy struck the family during the famine of 1876-78. Rama lost three of her family members within a few months, her sister, her father and her mother –the mother in the end. She and her elder brother, with the help of two villagers, had to carry her mother's body, when she was just 16 years old.

She and her elder brother again started to recite and sing scriptures near the temples, moving from one place to another. The range of her knowledge impressed people. When she was moving around in Calcutta, she was invited to speak before a few learned pandits. She impressed them so much that they gave her the title Pandita as well as another title Saraswati.

In Calcutta, Rama came in touch with the Brahmo Samaj people. There she was exposed to many religious ideas. The people of the Samaj encouraged her to learn more because they were interested in spreading women's education. They were happy to find someone like her. Keshab Chandra Sen suggested that she read Vedas and Upanishads, which she started doing.

In 1880, her brother too, the only surviving member of her family, died. Ramabai married her brother's friend, an active member of Brahmo Samaj who was from a Shudra caste. It was thus an inter-caste and inter-regional marriage. There was no support from his parents. Tragically, Ramabai's husband died just one and a half years after the marriage, leaving her with a daughter. At 23, Ramabai was a widow and a single mother. She decided to go back to Pune, her native place.

At the Brahmo Samaj, its leaders expected Ramabai to tell them that the scriptures were good and that they didn't oppose female education. Instead, Ramabai understood that the scriptures constantly disparaged women and heavily discriminated against them. She would be critical of the scriptures.

In Pune, Ramabai founded Arya Mahila Sabha in 1881. This was to promote education among women and to discourage child marriage. She wrote Stri Dharma Niti (Morals for Women) in 1882. She was promoting modern values, asking women to marry by choice and not marry early. In this way, Ramabai started the feminist discourse in India.

Ramabai gave testimony at the Hunter Commission of 1882. She told them there should be women teachers and women doctors, just like Phule wanted Shudra teachers. The cause of women's education needed to be promoted. Women were not going to male doctors, because of which their health problems were left untreated. Hunter was then invited to a meeting of 280 women. Ramabai said on the occasion, "In 99 cases out of 100, educated men of this country are opposed to female education and the proper position of women. If they observe the slightest fault, they magnify the grain of mustard seed into a mountain and try to ruin the character of a woman."

Ramabai herself planned to become a doctor. She started improving her English language for that purpose. Her book Stri Dharma Niti was doing well, and with the proceeds from its sales, she went to England in 1883 to study medicine. But sadly she was found ineligible, because of the deafness she developed in one ear during the famine. Instead of medicine, she joined a different field. She also got a job to teach the two languages she knew, Sanskrit and Marathi.

Soon after she went to England Ramabai got converted to Christianity, along with her daughter, and started signing her name as Mary Rama, retaining her Indian background. Ramabai had familiarised herself with Christianity during her Brahmo Samaj days. In England, she learnt a lot about the work of the sisters. She was impressed and surprised by the service motive of the sisters.

Later she gave reasons why she converted. She said, "Only two things on which all those books, the Dharma Shastras, the sacred epics, the Puranas and modern poets, the popular preachers of the present day and orthodox high-caste men, were agreed, that women of high and low caste, as a class were bad, very bad, worse than demons, as unholy as untruth; and they could not get moksha, as men."

No doubt her decision to covert would give her many problems, but she did it with a conviction. Ramabai did as a single woman what Ambedkar would do with thousands of followers many decades later. Both acted on their conscience with boldness in turning away from Hinduism.

Ramabai did not blindly accept the Christian faith, she was critical of it too, just as Ambedkar was critical of Buddhism that was in practice. In England, Ramabai was questioning things like the doctrine of the trinity, which refers to the belief in God, Jesus, and the Holy Spirit being three aspects of the Godhead. Ramabai also continued wearing Indian dress and remained vegetarian, and then she argued that the crucifix need not have a Latin inscription but it can be in Sanskrit!

The Anglican Church did not like Ramabai's sceptical attitude towards Christianity. They wanted her to have complete faith in the religion. But she said, "If I wanted to follow somebody's authority, I could have followed it before." The sisters there were critical of her mothering also. Ramabai was a woman of a firm and independent mindset.

From England, Ramabai went to the US in 1886, on an invitation to attend the graduation ceremony of her cousin who would be the first woman doctor from India. She wanted to stay in the US only for a few weeks, but there she got in touch with many people, and then she started giving lectures. She wrote the book The High Caste Hindu Woman in 1887. Her focus was on the higher caste because higher caste meant more orthodoxy and more problems for the women. Amazingly she wrote this book in English, a language she learnt only recently.

Ramabai interacted with the feminists in the US, and with the women who were freed from slavery. She formed Ramabai Association in 1887, to raise funds to start a widows' home in India. She evolved into a full-blown feminist thinker in America and gained some international recognition. She cultivated a network of friends and supporters. This was taking place a few years before 1893 when Vivekananda became popular in the US.

Ramabai came back to India in 1889. She wrote The People of the United States in Marathi, sharing her impressions of the US. She thought that India should emulate the US, while Vivekananda spoke about what the West could learn from the East. Ramabai particularly liked the people's consciousness of rights in America.

She liked the free and modern spirit of the country with a thriving civil society. When she said that that's how India should be too, she was envisioning an India which was free from British rule.

In 1889, Ramabai started Sharada Sadan in Bombay, which was later shifted to Pune. This was a secular residential school for high-caste widows. In 1889, she spoke at a Congress party meeting where out of 3000 delegates only three were women.

Opposition to her work

Many reformers like Ranade supported Ramabai's work for widows. But people had a problem with her conversion. Indian nationalists focused on how great we were, they approved of Vivekananda's approach of exalting Hinduism. But Ramabai was exposing the Indian culture before the British, the Americans, and the West.

Ramabai did not propagate Christianity though. She did not try to convert the widows at Sharada Sadan. Ramabai was Christian, her daughter was Christian, and they would pray with doors open. She was a kind of ideal woman to the people. If she was Christian and a great human being, it tempted people to think that Christianity was more helpful, and that was how many started taking to Christianity. The press called Sharada Sadan "Widows' mission house." And other social reformers disassociated with it slowly. Tilak was very critical of Ramabai, and Ranade also withdrew his support. Only Jyotiba Phule supported her. If it was not for Ramabai's Christianity, she would have gotten more recognition and support. But Ramabai was going by her convictions.

Sharada Sadan was later shifted to Kedgaon, a place a few kilometres away from Pune, because of the plague in the late 1890s. It came to be called Mukti Mission. Mukti Mission became much bigger than Sharada Sadan. Over 2000 women found refuge in it. Besides Hindu widows, there were also famine victims and sexually assaulted women. During the famine, Ramabai and her associates went to the affected areas and brought afflicted women to the Mission on ox carts. Many were brought though there was no proper accommodation to house so many people. There were many Dalit women too among the inmates.

The women occupied themselves with many activities. They were building the residential quarters themselves. They obtained the stone needed for construction from nearby. The women also did things like ploughing and gardening. They even ran a printing press. Ramabai believed in self-reliance. Education was expected to bring this self-reliance. The women were given basic education as well as training in many activities.

Mukti Mission also brought in some incapacitated women, such as blind women and old women. These women were kept in a separate section called Kripa. This was like the work of Mother Theresa, who used to take many destitutes. Christianity indeed provides a better framework for work with destitutes than any other religion.

In 1908, Ramabai embarked on translating the Bible into Marathi. There was already a Marathi translation, but that was more literary whereas Ramabai wanted the Bible to be written in a language that was closer to the language of lower-caste women. To understand the Bible in its original text, she started learning Hebrew and Greek. She got to know 7 languages in all. How did Ramabai pick up this kind of linguistic skill? It was probably because of her father's training in Sanskrit grammar. She might have been taught grammar in such a way that she knew the pattern of how languages were constituted. In this aspect, she was closer to Rammohan Roy.

In 1919, the government bestowed her the Kaiser-i-Hind award for her service to Indian education. Her daughter accepted this award because Ramabai was sick at this time. Tragically, her daughter died in 1921, at the age of 40. Ramabai was not even given the solace of dying by her daughter's side. She died the next year.

Mukti Mission is active today. Ramabai's bold and unusual life is worthy of reflection.

Think on it

1. What do you know about Ramabai's childhood?
2. What do you know about Ramabai's experience with the Brahmo Samaj?
3. What was Ramabai's position on the Hindu scriptures?
4. What was Ramabai's recommendation to the Hunter Commission?
5. Why did Ramabai convert to Christianity?
6. How did Ramabai come to be known in the US?
7. Why was there opposition to Ramabai's work in India?
8. What do you know about Mukti Mission?
9. Why do you think Ramabai is not well-known despite being a great person?

Swami Vivekananda

CHAPTER FIVE

Pride in Hinduism

Swami Vivekananda (1863–1902), born Narendranath Datta, studied Western philosophy and used to go to Brahmo Samaj meetings as a youngster. From his childhood, he had a fascination with becoming a wandering Hindu monk. He was keenly interested in religious matters. He used to ask the people who were coming to the Brahmo Samaj meetings whether any of them had seen God. No one could say, "Yes, I saw God," but somebody advised him that if he was really interested in meeting a saint, he should go to a priest at the Kali temple in Dakshineshwar. It was there that a young Narendranath met Ramakrishna Paramahamsa.

Ramakrishna Paramahamsa (1836–86) was a very spiritual person from his childhood. He had a profound experience of trance in his early childhood. We don't know what happens within during a trance – from the outside, one is motionless. As he grew up, he had more such trance experiences, and sometimes he would see the goddess Kali. He interacted with the people of many religious traditions and cults. He also deliberately took up the practice of different religions, including Islam. Through these varied practices, he came to understand that the paths of different religions and sects all lead to God.

Ramakrishna's approach was not based on thought and reason, it was more experiential. He attained the experience of spiritual ecstasy or the state of God-intoxication. He said that merely reading scriptures is like carrying tons of sugar but not tasting sweetness. He said that religion is not worth pursuing without having a direct experience of God.

Vivekananda approached this priest and asked him, have you seen God? Ramakrishna answered, "Yes, I see God just like I see you, but only more clearly." Vivekananda was awed by Ramakrishna's directness. He did not believe Ramakrishna at first, he thought this man was somewhat crazy. Still Vivekananda used to go to him and was gradually drawn to him. There used to be many discussions and arguments between them and in time Vivekananda became Ramakrishna's favourite disciple.

Differs with Brahmo Samaj

Vivekananda came to form views different from those of the Brahmo Samaj. To the people of Brahmo Samaj, only Vedanta was true, only the one formless God was true. They wanted nothing to do with various Hindu gods and avataras. Vivekananda saw it differently. Vivekananda came to believe that idol-worship can also be a way of reaching God, as Ramakrishna was worshipping idols, and he considered Ramakrishna to be an avatar. Religion is not simply a matter of reason but of experience. It can even be a revelation. It's about tasting sweetness.

Many people used to come to Ramakrishna, and some of them were well-read and scholarly. Keshab Chandra Sen was a well-known thinker of that time. He was struck by the originality and experience of this God-intoxicated man. He became instrumental in popularising Ramakrishna's teaching.

Vivekananda presented a new idea of Hinduism, which was nonetheless closer to the actual practice of Hindus unlike the Hinduism of the Brahmo Samaj. Vivekananda retains the centrality of Vedanta, it is the path of knowledge, but his approach doesn't negate various devotional paths. Ramakrishna realised through experience that all religions as well as various paths within Hinduism are diverse ways to reach God.

There was one saint by name Totapuri who asked Ramakrishna 'Why are you obsessed with Kali, why don't you see that God is formless?', and Totapuri helped Ramakrishna experience God as a formless presence. While God is formless, he can manifest in various forms too. Ramakrishna taught the validity of diverse religious and spiritual approaches. Vivekananda was convinced that this was the real spirit of Hinduism.

The presence of Ramakrishna Paramahamsa at that time in Bengal was a great blessing to India. Ramakrishna Paramahamsa was a manifestation of the ancient wisdom of India. He was an authentic proof of the worth of Hinduism. It was through the teachings of Ramakrishna and Vivekananda that many people in modern India could grasp the spiritual authenticity of Hinduism.

Vivekananda's experience with Ramakrishna made him understand a great deal about Hinduism. He soon came to be in a position to preach spirituality to the Western people. It was his speech at the Parliament of Religions in Chicago in 1893 and the subsequent series of lectures that made him popular in America and Europe. The fact that many Europeans and Americans were avidly listening to Vivekananda, a Hindu monk, made the people in India more confident in their religion. Vivekananda became an inspirational figure. He was like an explosion of Hindu pride.

Vivekananda looked at what was causing the backwardness of Indian society. He redefined the purpose of religion in a poor country like India. Against caste, he said: "All knowledge is in every soul regardless of caste order, the same power is in every man." Against untouchability, he said: "We are neither Vedantists, nor Puranics, nor Tantrics. We are 'don't touchists.' If this goes on for another century, every one of us will be in a lunatic asylum." "No religion on earth preaches the dignity of humanity in such a lofty strain as Hinduism, and no religion on earth treads upon the necks of the poor and the low in such a fashion as Hinduism."

Vivekananda was also providing a kind of new identity to India. "Look at the Western and other nations, which are now almost borne down, half-killed, and degraded by political ambitions." "Religion was the consideration in India, while politics, power, and even intellect from a secondary consideration." "Political greatness or military power will never be the mission of my race."

Why did India become like this, enslaved and impoverished? Vivekananda says that it became otherworldly because of its religion and lost its focus on material progress. "The medieval religious sects had created an unfortunate tendency to find salvation through escape from worldly experience." By focusing on the otherworldly, we missed the worldly. Vivekananda said that we should reverse this process. "You can't feed your own family, or dole out food to two of your fellowmen, you cannot do even an ordinary piece of work for the common good, in harmony with others, and you are running after mukti."

Unlike Roy, Vivekananda attributed a higher role to the society and people's sense of morality than to state and law in bringing about social change. He said, "No nation is great or good because Parliament enacts this or that, but because its men are great and good." "Men cannot be made virtuous by an act of Parliament and that is why religion is of deeper importance than politics, since, it goes to the root, deals with the essentials of conduct." When the state tries to control "through rigid laws and threats of punishment to follow that path with unconditional obedience the destiny of mankind becomes no better than that of a machine."

On law, Vivekananda said, "The very word sannyasin means the divine outlaw." "It is freedom alone that is desirable. It is not a law that we want but the ability to break the law. We want to be outlaws. If you are bound by laws, you will be a lump of clay." "Our aim should be to allow the individual to move towards this freedom. More of goodness, less of artificial law." In political thought, we commonly see what is a person's stand in the state vs society debate. Vivekananda is clearly on the side of society.

"In the days of famine and flood and disease and pestilence, tell me where your Congressmen are? Will it do to say, 'Hand over the government to us?' If there be two thousand people working in several districts, wont it be the turn of the English to consult you?" In those times when the Congress party was fighting for independence, Vivekananda wanted it to be more involved with the actual social work. He advocated voluntary action by committed individuals and groups for the upliftment of society.

What India needs most is education. Education can be a part of the social action by the people who are interested in the development of India. "The higher classes in India and America are the same but the distance is infinite between the lower classes between the two countries. When one great man dies, we must sit for centuries to have another, they can produce them as fast as they die. Why so? Because they have such a bigger field of recruiting their great ones, we have so small. Educate and raise the masses, thus alone a nation is possible."

Vivekananda believed that religion is not meant for academic speculation. And in the context of pre-independence India, the main purpose of religion is not to make people go in search of moksha, its main purpose is to motivate people to serve their fellowmen. Vivekananda established the Ramakrishna Mutt with social work as its primary focus.

Vivekananda also made certain observations on the nature of British rule. "For writing a few words of innocent criticism, men are being hurried to transportation for life; others imprisoned without trial and nobody knows when his head will be off. There has been a reign of terror in India for some years. English soldiers are killing our men and outraging our women – only to be sent home with passage and pension at our expense. We are in a terrible gloom- where is the Lord?"

What were Indians doing? "The highly educated and prominent men among you form themselves into societies and clamour at the top of their voices, 'O English rulers, admit our countrymen to the higher offices of the state, relieve us of famines and so on. This rendering of the air day and night with the eternal cry of 'Give' and 'Give'. The burden of all this speech is to give to us, give more to us..." Vivekananda thought that these educated Indians were more or less begging the British to change.

Egoistic nationalism

Vivekananda exalted service to the country, igniting patriotism in Indians. "I am grateful to the lands of the West for the many warm hearts that received me with all the love that pure and disinterested souls alone can give, but my life's allegiance is to this, my motherland and if I had a thousand lives, every moment of the whole series would be consecrated to your service, my countrymen."

"If foreign friends, you come with genuine sympathy to help and not to destroy, God speed to you. But if by abuses incessantly hurled against the head of a prostate race, you mean only the triumphant assertion of the moral superiority of your nation, let me tell you, the Hindu will be head and shoulders above all other nations in the world as a moral race."

Vivekananda's attitude would sometimes smack of egoistic nationalism that provoked national pride. It is the attitude of we will outdo you, we will outsmart you. Or sometimes he makes exaggerated statements like 'allegiance to India for the next thousand lives!' Such an attitude tends to blow up the egoism of the nation, and I don't think it's a healthy attitude, especially if spiritual people indulge in it.

Nor his analysis of the decline of India is accurate. Scientific and political developments in Europe contributed to the rise of the West, making India relatively backward. Not that Hindus became more spiritual and lost interest in material things and so became backward. Iqbal also attributed the backwardness of Muslims to their loss of interest in material things!

Father of modern India?

In 1933, a meeting was held to commemorate the death centenary of Rammohan Roy, in which Rabindranath Tagore, Sarvepalli Radhakrisnan, and Bipin Chandra Pal spoke of Rammohan Roy as the 'Father of Modern India.' By that, they may have meant Roy was the earliest to bring modern ideas to India. However, we have to consider if Vivekananda could be more worthy of the honour.

To be a father is to give birth to some entity, with an ego, with an ability to get hurt and an ability to take pride. After Vivekananda, you see a confident, resurgent, and assertive India with a clear identity. Although the pride in the motherland based on the Hindu religion could have contributed to the alienation of Muslims. Considering both positive and negative factors, I think Vivekananda may be considered the father of modern India for giving India an identity, an ego, and its specific sources of pride. You can reflect on this.

Think on it

1. What was Vivekananda like before he met Ramakrishna?
2. What do you know about the religious experiences of Ramakrishna Paramahamsa?
3. How was the approach of Ramakrishna to Hinduism different from that of Rammohan Roy?
4. How did Ramakrishna shape Vivekananda's views on Hinduism?
5. What is the historical significance of Ramakrishna Paramahamsa?
6. What were the evils of Hinduism that Vivekananda spoke against?
7. What according to Vivekananda should a Hindu monk do?
8. According to Vivekananda, in what ways should the Indian society be changed?
9. What was Vivekananda's suggestion for Congress?
10. What did Vivekananda say about the nature of British rule?
11. Did Vivekananda create pride in the motherland among Indians?

Balagangadhar Tilak

CHAPTER SIX

Swaraj Is a Birthright – Only for Upper-Caste Hindu Males?

Balagangadhar Tilak (1856–1920), a Marathi Chitpavan Brahmin, was one of the top leaders in India's struggle for independence before the Gandhian era. He is also known as Lokmanya, which meant 'respected by people'. Around that time the Congress people were divided into moderates and extremists. The moderates had the upper hand from 1885 to 1907. The methods used by the moderates were the three Ps, as the extremists called them: petition, prayer and protest. Balagangadhar Tilak, Lala Lajpat Rai and Bipin Chandra Pal, who were called Lal-Bal-Pal, proposed different methods, methods of non-cooperation, civil disobedience, and boycott. These are the same methods that Gandhi would use later.

Tilak famously proclaimed, "Swaraj is my birthright and I shall have it." Tilak was a leader of the extremists. He distinguished his position from that of moderates in this way: "At present, we are clerks and willing instruments of our own oppression in the hands of an alien government. What the New Party wants you to do is to realise the fact that your future rests entirely in your own hands. Boycott is a political weapon. We shall not give them assistance to collect revenue and keep peace. We shall not assist them in fighting beyond the frontiers or outside India with Indian blood and money. We shall not assist them in carrying on the administration of justice. We shall have our own courts, and when the time comes we shall not pay taxes. Can you do that by your united efforts? If you can, you are free from tomorrow" (1907).

Tilak was a little ahead of his times as the methods Tilak advocated would be used years later. Unfortunately, this is the only positive thing about him. Tilak's nationalism and his views on various other things were extremely narrow-minded. If people like Tilak had led the movement further, it would have fared far worse. Fortunately, Gandhi came and took over the charge from Tilak and India was saved.

Support to terrorism

Tilak justified terrorism, that is, the use of violence for political gains. He said that the Bhagavad Gita supports using violence for a right cause. Tilak was imprisoned twice for his alleged support to terrorist activities. Had more people followed terrorist methods, inspired by Tilak, there would have been a great deal of violence.

Tilak gave ideological support to the killing of the British officers by Chapekar brothers in 1897, because of which he was imprisoned for 18 months. Charged with sedition, Tilak was jailed for the second time in 1908, for six years. He was defending Prafulla Chaki and Khudiram Bose who threw a bomb to kill an officer but killed two women instead. Tilak was charged again in 1916, but his lawyer, Jinnah, could successfully defend him this time though he couldn't do it earlier in 1908.

When charged with sedition, Tilak argued he was innocent. After the judgement in 1908 Tilak said, "All I wish to say is that in spite of the verdict of the jury, I maintain that I am innocent. There are higher powers that rule the destiny of things and it may be the will of Providence that the cause which I represent may prosper more by my suffering than by remaining free." Years later, when charged with sedition, Gandhi would plead guilty and seek punishment! And Jinnah could never understand such a method!

Communalism

In 1894, it was Tilak who transformed Ganesha festival into a public event consisting of several days of processions. The festival was turned into an occasion to promote solidarity among the Hindus. Tilak also asked the Hindus not to participate in Muharram celebrations, as they used to do at that time. In 1895, Tilak initiated celebrating the birth anniversary of Shivaji. He organised a fund to reconstruct Shivaji tomb at Raigad Fort. Shivaji was only a Hindu hero who resisted the Moghuls and gave them great trouble. A Hindu hero was made a national hero. Tilak's people used to urge the Hindus to protect cows, Tilak wanted a ban on beef consumption by Muslims. Such things became a source of communal tensions. The Muslim League grew from 1906 onwards.

On women

Tilak's views on women and caste were shockingly regressive. Indian textbooks explained that Tilak believed in political reform first and social reform next, but in reality Tilak was opposed to social reform.

Tilak opposed the starting of a girls' high school in Pune in 1885, where his newspapers were used as part of the curriculum. There was an incident involving a girl Rukhma who got married at the age of 11 but refused to go to her husband. The husband went to the court and in 1887 the court ordered the little girl, based on Hindu scriptures, to go to her husband or face six months of imprisonment. The girl still refused to go to her husband and was ready to face the punishment. Tilak supported the interpretation of Hindu scriptures, endorsing the judgement. The interpretation might be right, but do you want such scriptures is an issue. The marriage was later dissolved by the intervention of Queen Victoria herself. Rukhmabai went on to become a doctor from the London School of Medicine.

In 1889, a 10-year-old girl Phulmoni Dasi died because of forceful sex by her 35-year-old husband. A rape charge could not be brought against the husband, but he was found guilty of causing death due to negligence. Such incidents led to the Age of Consent Act of 1891, which increased the minimum age of girls to be married from 10 to 12. Though this was a marginal improvement, even that much of a change was strongly opposed by Tilak. Tilak blamed the girl for having "defective female organs," He called her one of those "dangerous freaks of nature."

On caste

Tilak opposed inter-caste marriages, particularly those between upper-caste women and lower-caste men. He also refused to sign a petition for the abolition of untouchability in 1918, though he himself spoke against the practice of untouchability earlier.

In another case, the Maratha rulers had been asking the Brahmins to grant them a Kshatriya status, but the Brahmins refused to do it and continued to treat them as Shudras. This was particularly resented by Shahu, the ruler of the princely state of Kolhapur, who was influenced by Phule and who would go on to help Ambedkar in his fight against the suppression of the lower castes. Tilak however supported the Brahmins.

A British historian of colonial India, Gordon Johnson wrote this on Tilak: "It is significant that even at the time when Tilak was making political use of Shivaji the question of conceding Kshatriya status to him as Maratha was resisted by the conservative Brahmins including Tilak. While Shivaji was a brave man, all his bravery did not give him the right to a status that very nearly approached that of a Brahman."

Tilak's nationalism did not include Muslims but only Hindus. And his Hinduism did not care either for Hindu women or for the lower castes among the Hindus. His nationalism is that narrow. But he is proud of his Hinduism. Tilak had a high opinion of Vivekananda, who contributed to the pride in Hinduism. He said, "No Hindu, who, has the interests of Hinduism at his heart, could help feeling grieved over Vivekananda's samadhi. Vivekananda, in short, had taken the work of keeping the banner of Advaita philosophy forever flying among all the nations of the world and made them realise the true greatness of Hindu religion and Hindu people. Thousands of years ago, Shankaracharya showed to the world the glory and greatness of Hinduism. Vivekananda is second

Shankaracharya."

Think on it

1. What was the difference between moderates and extremists in the Indian independence movement?
2. What was Tilak's stand on terrorism?
3. What was the difference between Tilak's stand and Gandhi's stand when charged with sedition?
4. What were Tilak's actions that contributed to communalism?
5. What were Tilak's views on caste?
6. What were Tilak's views on gender differences?

Mahatma Gandhi

CHAPTER SEVEN

An Ethical Approach to Politics

Mahatma Gandhi (1869–1948) was a great moral force in the field of politics. His approach to politics, we can say, is deeply moral. It is also spiritual and religious. Gandhi doesn't make any distinction between spirituality and religion. To him, religion and politics are closely intertwined. Modern India is a secular democracy based on the concept of separation of state and religion, but for Gandhi religion is integral to politics. He asserted: "I can say without the slightest hesitation, and yet in all humility, that those who say that religion has nothing to do with politics do not know what religion means." For most politicians, politics is a power game, but to Gandhi politics means spiritual practice and religious work.

Political, economic, social, spiritual and religious dimensions are all interrelated for Gandhi. 'Swaraj' – meaning a free country – is the term Gandhi uses for his ideal society. He says, "The square of swaraj has four sides – the political, the economic, the social and dharma." Some people may question if we bring religion into politics, wouldn't it lead to conflict between the various religions? Some may want to bring in Hinduism, some Islam, and some Christianity. How does Gandhi tackle this problem?

Gandhi defines religion very broadly, it is not just about a set of beliefs and rituals. Hinduism is not about the various gods and temples etc. to Gandhi, it is about something more philosophical. He said that Hinduism is a "search after truth through non-violent means." He finds his core principles, truth and non-violence in Hinduism. His notion of religion is highly interpretative and is far from empirical or scholarly. Gandhi would say this is what religion means to me, whether scholars or other people agree or not.

The Bhagavad Gita is one scripture that is closest to Gandhi's heart. It is spiritual teaching set on the battlefield. It seems like a clear exhortation of violence. But to Gandhi, the Gita doesn't teach violence. He says, "But to say that the Gita teaches or justifies war is as wrong as to say that violence is the law of life. The field of battle is our own body. An eternal battle is going on between the two camps of higher impulse and lower impulse. Krishna is the dweller within, ever whispering in a pure heart." So the Pandavas and the Kauravas, the two sides on the battlefield, are just higher and lower impulses in the mind. There have been hundreds of commentaries on the Gita, but no one has interpreted the Gita in a purely symbolical sense like this.

Gandhi says, "Hinduism is not an exclusive religion. In it, there is room for the worship of all the prophets of the world. Hinduism tells everyone to worship God according to his own faith or Dharma so it lives at peace with the religions." So a Muslim can freely pray to Allah, and a Christian can pray to Jesus. Traditionally, Hinduism has indeed been a more tolerant religion because it evolved by absorbing many tribal deities and customs, but to say that it tells everyone to worship God according to his own faith is not a common interpretation of Hinduism.

Gandhi thinks that there are certain common values across the religions, and he seeks to bring them into politics. Gandhi's core value seems to be selflessness or even self-sacrifice – working tirelessly for the good of others. He says, "Our desires and motives may be divided into two classes – selfish and unselfish. All selfish desires are immoral, while the desire to improve ourselves for the sake of doing good to others is truly moral. The highest moral law is that we should unremittingly work for the good of mankind."

Simple living

Gandhi extended his values in political and social spheres to the economy too. Unselfishness has economic aspects as well. He famously said that there is enough on the earth for everyone's need but not for anyone's greed. To Gandhi, we should only seek to satisfy our basic needs and should lead a life of simplicity.

Especially when there are so many poor people around, it is very unethical to seek to accumulate wealth for oneself and live a luxurious life. Gandhi says, "Under the new outlook, a multiplicity of material wants will not be the aim of life, the aim will be rather their restriction consistently with comfort. We shall cease to think of getting what we can, but we shall decline to receive what all can't get" (What of the West, 1925). This could be a powerful economic ideal based on the concept of equality. Refusing for oneself what everyone else cannot get means being willing to live with just the minimal necessities.

But could one be happy living this way? To Gandhi, the answer is yes. This is similar to the Socratic position that virtue and happiness go together. Socrates, Plato and Aristotle believed in the unity of ethics and happiness. In a way, Gandhi is bringing this notion back, though his ethics might not have been the same as their ethics. A common person seeks to maximise his own pleasure and happiness, but Gandhi thinks that true happiness can only come through doing the opposite, through self-sacrifice and selflessness.

Gandhi explicitly rejects the utilitarian principle of maximising happiness: "I do not believe in the doctrine of the greatest good of the greatest number. It means in its nakedness that in order to achieve the supposed good of 51 per cent the interest of 49 per cent maybe, or rather, should be sacrificed. It is a heartless doctrine and has done harm to humanity. The only real, dignified, human doctrine is the greatest good of all, and this can only be achieved by uttermost self-sacrifice." To Gandhi, it will not do if just the majority is happy, every single person should be happy and anyone who lives by ethics should strive to see to it, even at the cost of giving up one's happiness. Such sacrifice itself can be a source of deeper happiness.

Gandhi thinks that an ideal society comes into being when the people have an idea of not only their rights but also of their duties – duty to lead a simple life, duty to resist evil, duty to contribute to a better economic, political and social system and so on. "Most people do not understand the complicated machinery of the government. They do not realise every citizen silently but nonetheless certainly sustains the government of the day in ways of which he has no knowledge. Every citizen, therefore, renders himself responsible for every act of his government. And it is quite proper to support it so long as the actions of the government are bearable. But when they hurt him and his nation it becomes his duty to withdraw his support."

Think on it

1. What is a religion to Gandhi?
2. Why does not Gandhi separate religion from politics?
3. What is Gandhi's interpretation of the Gita?
4. Why is Hinduism more tolerant of various beliefs and gods?
5. Does ethical living bring happiness, according to Gandhi?
6. Why is Gandhi against utilitarian thinking?
7. Why are duties as important as rights?
8. Do you agree with mixing religion and politics? What could the dangers be?

CHAPTER EIGHT

Satyagraha

The concept of Satyagraha is a very important contribution to the political thought by Gandhi. It is essentially about a nonviolent way of defying authority. The word 'satya' in Sanskrit means truth and 'agraha' means force, so etymologically the word 'satyagraha', coined by Gandhi himself, means truth-force. Truth and nonviolence are core values for Gandhi. Truth is supposed to exist within every human being, even in an enemy because of which he can be transformed. Truth signifies the potential for transformation. Sometimes this truth is equated with God. Seeking truth means the same thing as seeking God.

And God is also love. Nonviolence, in its broadest sense as used by Gandhi, meant love – even for the enemy. Gandhi said, "In its negative form, ahimsa means not injuring any living being whether by body or mind. In its positive form, ahimsa means love. I must love my enemy as I would my wrong-doing father or son." When you disagree with the opinions or actions of your father, usually you would want to change him and his way of thinking but you wouldn't hate him for that. This should be the attitude of a Satyagrahi.

But one has to remember that one doesn't have a monopoly over truth, as in the validity of a viewpoint. Your opponent or superior too may also have some truth on his side, he may have a valid point of view too. In satyagraha, you are not trying to impose your viewpoint on the other by force, you are only trying to bring his attention to see the validity of your viewpoint. Maybe in this process, you would also be able to see the other's viewpoint in a better way. Gandhi's resistance to authority is a kind of deeper communication.

Gandhi only wants to convince his enemy about the validity of his demand, gently and patiently. He said, "In the application of Satyagraha, I discovered in the earliest stages that pursuit of Truth did not admit of violence being inflicted on one's opponent, but that he must be weaned from error by patience and sympathy. For what appears to be Truth to the one may appear false to the other."

People who are resisting an act of imposition of authority in a nonviolent way can do it in many ways, such as through demonstrations, protests and fasting. Violence means inflicting pain on the other but nonviolence implies a willingness to suffer. A Satyagrahi is willing to suffer physically rather than make the enemy suffer. This suffering may mean accepting physical violence or going on a fast.

Suffering plays a vital part in the resistance, in convincing your opponent. Gandhi said, "I have found that mere appeal to reason does not answer where prejudices are age-long and based on supposed religious authority. Reason has to be strengthened by suffering." Gandhi elevates the concept of suffering to a new level. One should be willing to go through such intense suffering as to melt the enemy's heart. Gandhi said, "Suffering is the law of human beings; war is the law of the jungle. The appeal of the reason is more to the head, but the penetration of the heart comes from suffering. It opens up the inner understanding of men."

A person who is involved in Satyagraha is expected to be not only just but also transparent both in his demands and actions. "All his actions must be transparent through and through. Diplomacy and intrigue can have no place in his armoury."

Gandhi launched Non-cooperation Movement, Civil Disobedience, and Quit India movements. The lakhs of people who participated in these mass movements might not have had much understanding of Gandhi's philosophy, some of them might not have realised even the significance of nonviolence. Early on, Gandhi launched a movement against the Rowlatt Act which turned violent. The Non-cooperation Movement also turned violent at one stage, and Gandhi had to discontinue it. The Civil Disobedience Movement went well, but the Quit India Movement was more spontaneous and chaotic. Many people were jailed.

Many people participated in the Gandhian movements not because they were convinced by any spiritual reasons, but they saw it as a pragmatic way to resist an authority with far superior military power than them. Gandhi too wielded his Satyagraha movements like a political weapon. Nonviolence has several advantages over violence while facing a much superior enemy. It also enables mass participation.

Discipline is needed for this kind of movement. He said, "The nation must be disciplined to handle mass movements in a sober and methodical manner. We can do no effective work unless we can pass instructions to the crowd and expect implicit obedience." The Non-cooperation Movement had to be stopped at one stage because it became "a mob without a mind."

Gandhi's method of mobilisation enabling mass participation for a just cause was historically appropriate. It worked in India, though we cannot say it would work in every circumstance. To Gandhi, the concept of nonviolence or ahimsa embodied a whole philosophy, but he did not expect everyone to understand it. He said, "Ahimsa with me is a creed, the breath of life. It is never as a creed that I placed it before India. I placed it before the Congress as a political weapon, to be employed for the solution of practical problems."

Think on it

1. What is the wider meaning of nonviolence?
2. What should be the attitude of a Satyagrahi towards his enemy?
3. Why should a Satyagrahi be willing to suffer?

4. Why were the Gandhian methods of nonviolence more appropriate during British rule?

CHAPTER NINE

Swaraj – the Ideal Political System

Gandhi believed in a particular economic and political system which he called swaraj. We can compare the philosophy underpinning it with the philosophy of liberal democracy to see what they have in common and how they differ.

To Gandhi, individual liberty is of utmost importance. And that liberty includes the scope to resist when the government is being unfair. Liberty is an individual right, but resisting any unfair policy of the government is an individual's duty, and both rights and duties go together. This kind of liberty is essential for the functioning of Gandhi's ideal political system, the swaraj.

Gandhi strongly opposed socialist systems that did not respect individuality, that tried to kill individuality to promote equality. At the same time, Gandhi is against blatant inequalities that arise in a democracy. He wouldn't support Western democracies because they have generated extreme inequalities. Gandhi is very much for economic equality, but to him, it is not based on any socialist agenda, it simply means that "everybody should have enough for his or her needs." Gandhi promotes the ideal of a simple life, it looked very odd to him that somebody could enjoy the luxuries of a wealthy life while thousands around him are starving. However, Gandhi does not want to achieve economic equality by encroaching on an individual's freedom, but only by appealing to his moral sensibilities.

Gandhi says socialist governments do "the greatest harm by destroying individuality." He gives the greatest importance to the individual. "The individual is the one supreme consideration. If the individual ceases to count, what is left of society?" Gandhi is for economic equality but in his swaraj there is no abolition of private property. Private property may promote inequalities, but it is still much better than forcibly imposing equality. "The violence of the private property is less injurious than the violence of the state."

So Gandhi is against capitalism and all the selfishness and greed it engenders, but he is not for a socialist system. Capitalism should be restrained, but not by force. It should be restrained only by promoting ethical values."If the state suppressed capitalism by violence, it will be caught in the coils of violence itself and fail to develop non-violence at any time." For Gandhi, nonviolence is a great value because it gives the scope to individual to live his life in freedom without any fear.

Thus, despite being a great champion of economic equality, Gandhi had the great insight to see the potential evil of a socialist state. "I look upon an increase in the power of State with the greatest fear, because although while apparently doing good by minimising exploitation, it does the greatest harm to mankind by destroying individuality which lies at the root of all progress." If he has to choose between equality and individuality, Gandhi clearly gives greater preference to individuality.

So Gandhi is against the socialist state and is for democracy, but democracy comes with its own dangers. It is a threat to individuality in its own way, and Gandhi has qualms about it. He fears the oppression of majoritarianism, it has no place in his swaraj. "Let us not push the mandate theory to ridiculous extremes and become slaves to resolutions of majorities. Swaraj will be an absurdity if individuals have to surrender their judgement to the majority." Democracy can thrive only when individuals are capable of resisting the sway of the majority because the majority can be wrong too.

In Gandhi's swaraj, every individual has a voice. The swaraj safeguards freedom of speech, and dissident individuals are protected. Your views can be different from others' views and you should feel free to express them. Gandhi's views on free speech are similar to those of J S Mill. Gandhi says, "It has always been my experience that I am always true from my point of view and often wrong from the point of view of my honest critics. I know that we are both right from our respective points of view. And this knowledge saves me from attributing motives to my opponents or critics. I very much like the doctrine of the manyness of reality. It is this doctrine that has taught me to judge a Mussulman from his own standpoint and a Christian from his." There has to be room for plurality, there has to be tolerance for others' viewpoints and attitudes. "Intolerance is itself a form of violence and an obstacle to the growth of a true democratic spirit."

Gandhi evolved his philosophy of an ideal society during the freedom struggle while fighting the British. So civil disobedience is a major element of his philosophy. The British were a foreign government, but any government can turn oppressive and the people should have a right to protest. The people have to protect their freedom, and every individual's right to freedom has to be upheld. Gandhi says: "No society can possibly be built on the denial of individual freedom. It is contrary to the very nature of man. Just as a man will not grow horns or a tail, so will he not exist as a man if he has no mind of his own."

India can get freedom from the British, but real freedom can only happen when the masses are educated. "Real swaraj will come not by the acquisition of authority by a few but by the acquisition of the capacity by all to resist authority when it is abused. In other words, swaraj is to attained by educating the masses to a sense of their capacity to regulate and control authority."

So Gandhi is all for liberal democracy and individual rights, but the inequalities that can develop in such a democracy are a great cause of concern for him. He urged great caution against democracy deteriorating into fascism and imperialism. "My notion of democracy is that under it the weakest should have the same opportunity as the strongest. That can never happen except through non-violence. No country in the world today shows any but patronising regard for the weak. The land is owned by few capitalists. These large holdings can't be sustained except by violence, veiled if not open. Western democracy as it functions today is diluted Nazism or Fascism. At best it is merely a cloak to hide the Nazi and the fascist tendencies of imperialism" (1940).

On village

Gandhi's democracy consists of village republics. The village assumes central importance in Gandhi's swaraj. This ideal village is more or less politically independent and economically self-sufficient.

Gandhi thinks a typical Indian village can become a great example of a working democracy. But in reality, Gandhi's ideal village is hard to achieve in Indian conditions because of the prevalence of the caste system, just to begin with. Ambedkar was very much opposed to Gandhi's idealisation of rural life. To Ambedkar, a typical Indian village is a place of horrors, it is a den of most abhorrent forms of casteism. For thousands of years in India, village life fostered extreme inequalities along caste lines, there had been all kinds of discrimination and untouchability – so how can all of that be suddenly abrogated? How can there be a democracy? If an Indian village is left to itself in the interests of political independence, it will invariably remain dominated by the upper castes.

Gandhi's view of economic self-sufficiency is very problematic too. Gandhi believes in village-level production and village-level distribution, but that leads to a very primitive economy. Without trade and specialisation, there cannot be surplus and growth. Gandhi completely ignores this simple fact.

We live in an age of industry and technology, but Gandhi is opposed to heavy machinery. He thinks that heavy machinery displaces labour when there are already large numbers of unemployed labour, especially in the villages. Gandhi advocates the use of simple technology which he thinks will give more scope for employment. But in reality, the use of advanced technology coupled with trade can provide more and more employment for people in villages, with many better-paid jobs – but Gandhi seems to be ignorant of this possibility.

Gandhi simply says that mechanisation is "an evil when there are more hands than required for the work as is the case in India." Gandhi's simple solution for economic self-sufficiency of villages is the production of a form of cotton cloth called khadi, through a very primitive tool called spinning wheel. He envisages lakhs of villages across the country full of people constantly working to produce cotton cloth. He says, "Khadi is the only true economic proposition in terms of the millions of villages until such a time, if ever, when a better system of supplying work and adequate wages for every able-bodied person above the age of sixteen, male or female, is found for his field, cottage or even factory in every village of India."

Gandhi vehemently opposes central planning, which would be embraced by Nehru after independence. Gandhi wants every village to work out its particular situation. That is his idea of democracy. "True democracy cannot be worked by twenty men sitting at the Centre. It has to be worked from below by the people of every village." Mechanisation, technology, industrialisation, centralised production – these are all evil in Gandhi's view simply because he thinks they would rob people of jobs. "An intelligent plan will find the cottage method fit into the scheme for our country. Any planning in our country that ignores the absorption of labour wealth will be misplaced. The centralized method of production, whatever may be its capacity to produce, is incapable of finding employment for as large number of persons as we have to provide for. Therefore, it stands condemned in this country."

There can be many ways to look after the welfare of workers in an industrial setting but Gandhi simply does not want to consider them. He denies any possible scope for industrialisation, saying "No amount of socialism can eradicate the evils inherent in industrialism." This is so because he thinks that industrialisation inherently tends to deprive people of work, with machines gradually replacing people in everything, and nothing can be done to stop it.

Also, Gandhi advocated a very simple lifestyle for everyone, and he was against modern consumerism. In our times of looming climate crisis, Gandhi's firm stance against rampant consumerism is relevant. But we should welcome both technology and trade that can reduce greenhouse gas emissions.

Think on it

1. What are Gandhi's views on Indian villages?
2. Why is Ambedkar opposed to Gandhi's views on Indian villages?
3. Would Nehru agree with Gandhi's views on politically independent villages?
4. Why was Gandhi against heavy machinery?
5. Are Gandhi's views relevant in the context of climate change?

Rabindranath Tagore

CHAPTER TEN

The Power of the Spirit

"We must never forget in the present day that those people who have got their political freedom are not necessarily free, they are merely powerful." -- Rabindranath Tagore, (as quoted in The White Umbrella: Indian Political Thought from Manu to Gandhi by Brown D Mackenzie, 1953.)

Rabindranath Tagore (1861–1941) was a rare and extraordinary human being who thought of contemporary issues in a completely different way from others. Tagore was far ahead of his times. To Tagore, it was not just the Indians and other subjects of colonialism who were unfree, the rulers themselves, the British too, were unfree in their way. Because to Tagore, true freedom meant not just political freedom but freedom of mind. This freedom is an awakening, a release from darkness and ignorance. People of his time were fighting for the political freedom of India, but he envisioned much greater freedom for his country.

Where the mind is without fear and the head is held high
Where knowledge is free
Where the world has not been broken up into fragments
By narrow domestic walls
Where words come out from the depth of truth
Where tireless striving stretches its arms towards perfection
Where the clear stream of reason has not lost its way
Into the dreary desert sand of dead habit

Where the mind is led forward by thee
Into ever-widening thought and action
Into that heaven of freedom, my Father, let my country awake.

This well-known verse from his book Gitanjali (1912) expresses his vision of a free world. How did Tagore look at India's freedom struggle of that time? Did Tagore appreciate Gandhi's ideology? Did Tagore think that Gandhi was fighting for the kind of swaraj that Tagore himself wanted? It would seem like Tagore fully approved of Gandhi and his ideology. It was Tagore who first called Gandhi mahatma. Tagore supported Gandhi's nonviolent approach to the freedom struggle. Tagore thought that this was India's path, not just Gandhi's. There were quite a few differences between Gandhi and Tagore, but they were of lesser significance compared to the agreement they had on many issues.

Involvement in the freedom struggle

Tagore himself took part in the Swadeshi movement, but he retired from active politics around 1907-8. Tagore's grandfather Dwarakanath was a wealthy landlord and a close friend of Raja Rammohan Roy. Tagore went to study in England in 1879 when he was around 18 years of age. Back in India, he got involved in politics and then in social work for some years. Tagore first met Gandhi in 1915, Gandhi was eight years younger than Tagore. Gandhi had just returned from South Africa. Tagore was world-famous by then, having received the Nobel Prize for literature in 1913, and Gandhi too was already famous for fighting for the cause of Indians in South Africa.

Tagore had been in touch with Gandhi's activities in South Africa, through C F Andrews who was a mutual friend. Tagore didn't like the Swadeshi movement that was started in 1905 by Tilak and others. He didn't like the coercive methods used in the Swadeshi movement against those Indians who defied the boycott call, which involved stopping essential services like those of the barber and the washerman and beating up the people on the roads.

Tagore spoke against the use of threat and violence, "We could not bear the delay involved in gradually winning the consent of the people. The use of threat to stop dissent can't be called nationalistic unification" (1908).

Tagore then got involved in social work in villages on his estates. He helped set up free health centres, primary schools, night schools for adults, and a rural bank. He was distressed by the evils of the caste system, which were hindering his work. He realised the ground reality of Hindu society. He wrote, "Having seen all this, I no longer feel any desire to 'idealise' the Hindu samaj through delusions pleasant to the ear but ultimately suicidal."

Coming from an upper-caste landlord family, what are his views on inequalities? In a letter to his son who was abroad studying agriculture, Tagore wrote "Remember that the landlord's wealth is of the peasant. They are bearing the cost of your education by starving or half-starving themselves. It is your responsibility to repay this debt in full. That is the first task, even before the welfare of your own family." This is Marxism in a nutshell but Tagore's concern is based on compassion.

Tagore himself could not go ahead with his social work or political activism, but then came Gandhi. "Mahatma Gandhi came and stood at the cottage door of the destitute millions, clad as one of themselves, and talking to them in their own language." Addressing Gandhi, Tagore said, "You stood among us to proclaim your faith in the ideal which you know to be that of India, the ideal which is both against the cowardliness of hidden revenge and the cowed submissiveness of the terror-stricken." Tagore saw Gandhi as a saviour of the people.

Tagore believed that the power of spirit is higher than material or political power. India needed this force of good in fighting against the British. "This power of good must prove its truth and strength by its fearlessness, by its refusal to accept any imposition." There would be great suffering, but India must not lose its faith. "India must willingly accept her penance of suffering, the suffering which is the crown of the great. Armed with her utter faith in goodness, she must stand unabashed before the arrogance that scoffs at the power of the spirit." In victory or defeat, one needs to stand by the inner truth. "Those who believe in spiritual life know that to stand against wrong, which has overwhelming material power behind it is victory itself, it is the victory of the active faith in the ideal in the teeth of evident defeat."

Fear of violence

Before he launched his nationwide agitation against the Rowlatt Act, on April 5, 1919, Gandhi wrote to Tagore, "I will not be happy until I have received your considered opinion on this endeavour to purify the political country." On April 12, Tagore replied, addressing Gandhi as 'Dear Mahatmaji', "Passive resistance is a force which is not necessarily moral in itself; it can be used against truth as well as for it. The danger inherent in all force grows stronger when it is likely to gain success, for then it becomes a temptation." Tagore was cautioning Gandhi, expressing his reservations.

Gandhi too believed in the power of spirit, he wanted to fight evil not with evil but the with force of good. Still, it was not an easy thing to do. Tagore wrote to Gandhi, "Such a fight is for heroes and not for men led by impulses of the moment. Evil on one side naturally begets evil on the other, injustices leading to violence and insult to vengefulness." Gandhi too was concerned that his mass movement might turn violent, as indeed it did in Ahmedabad, Gandhi's own city, and other places, a few days before the Jalianwala Bagh event. In a letter to his secretary, Gandhi lamented, "In the place I have made my abode I find utter lawlessness bordering almost on Bolshevism. Englishmen and women have found it necessary to leave their bungalows and to confine themselves to a few well-guarded houses. I over-calculated the measure of permeation of satyagraha among the people. I underrated the power of hatred and ill will."

'Bolshevism' is a reference to the October Revolution of Russia. Gandhi's call against the Rowlatt Act, his very first implementation of Satyagraha, turned out to be a disaster. Tagore's fears turned out to be true.

Gandhi and Tagore thought very alike, in fact, Tagore seems to be even more idealistic than Gandhi. For Tagore, the spirit came above all. He said: "If we can defy the strong, the armed, the wealthy, revealing to the world power of the immortal spirit, the whole castle of the Giant Flesh will vanish in the void. And then Man will find his swaraj. We, the famished, ragged ragamuffins of the East, are to win freedom for all Humanity." The spirit will triumph, and the meek will inherit the earth, even as Jesus predicted: "The day was sure to come, when the frail man of spirit, completely unhampered by arms and air fleets and dreadnoughts will prove that the meek is to inherit the earth."

To Tagore, Gandhi embodied this spirit: "It is in the fitness of things that Mahatma Gandhi, frail in body and devoid of all material resources, should call up the immense power of the meek, that has been lying waiting in the heart of the destitute and the insulted humanity of India."

We live in a materialistic age. Tagore was not at all against material progress, we must learn many things about science and technology from the West. But at the same time, the East has something to give to the West too. Eventually, the West will find solace in the spirituality of the East. "The present age has powerfully been possessed by the West. It has only become possible because to her is given some great mission for man. We from the East have to come to her to learn whatever she has to teach us, for by doing so we hasten the fulfilment of this age. We know that the East has her lessons to give and she has her own responsibility of not allowing her light to be extinguished, and the time will come when the West will find leisure to realise that she has a home of hers in the East where her food is and her rest." Meanwhile, the East should not lose itself by going after power and wealth!

Think on it

1. Why would even the British be unfree, according to Tagore, though they were the rulers?
2. What is Tagore's notion of freedom?
3. What is the power of the spirit?
4. What were Tagore's fears of Gandhi's Satyagraha movement turning violent?
5. What are Tagore's views on the mutual influence of the East and the West?

CHAPTER ELEVEN

A Stance Against Nationalism

Tagore was one of the earliest critics of nationalism in this country. At that time, patriotism or nationalism was equated with anti-colonialism and was promoted vigorously. Although Tagore was against colonial exploitation, he was not convinced that nationalism was the right kind of thing for India. This was partly because around that time nationalism was responsible for, as Tagore saw it, the First World War and a possible Second World War. Tagore saw those developments as the advent of a new kind of evil, which India had to guard against. Tagore also felt that many wrong things could be justified in the name of nationalism, as his experience with the Swadeshi movement showed him.

In his Bengali novel Ghare Baire, written in 1915, one character by the name of Nikhilesh allows the sale of foreign cloth in his shop, though he doesn't wear them. He says, "I will not oppress." He doesn't want to oppress anyone who wants to buy foreign cloth. When his wife, influenced by another character in the novel, says, "The oppression is not for yourself, it is for the country," he replies, "Oppressing for the country is oppressing the country. You will not understand this." Tagore had the vision to foresee that in the name of the country many bad things would be done.

Tagore had misgivings about the non-cooperation movement, though he had a very high opinion of Gandhi. Gandhi's movement was promoting this sentiment of hatred against the British, which would be a sentiment against foreigners. Tagore could not be a part of the movement. In 1920, he wrote in a letter to C F Andrews, "I find our countrymen are furiously excited about non-cooperation. I shall be willing to sit at his [Gandhi's] feet and do his biddings if he commands me to cooperate with my countrymen in the service of love. I refuse to waste my manhood in lighting the fire of anger and spreading it from house to house."

Touring Europe, Tagore wrote in 1921, "What irony of fate is this that I should be preaching cooperation of cultures between East and West on this side of the sea just at the moment when the doctrine of non-cooperation is preached on the other side." Tagore was in Europe to collect funds to build an international centre of learning, Viswa Bharati, at Santiniketan. Tagore wrote, "I am striving with all my power to tune my mood of mind to be in accord with the great feeling of excitement sweeping across my country." But it seems like it was not happening.

Tagore thought that education should promote an international outlook and unity of mankind. In 1917, he wrote, "It is my conviction that my countrymen will truly gain their India by fighting the education which teaches them that a country is greater than the ideals of humanity."

Tagore had a personal meeting with Gandhi on 6 September 1921. Gandhi wanted to persuade Tagore to take a public stand and fight for swaraj. Tagore said, "The whole world is suffering today from the cult of a selfish and short-sighted nationalism." Gandhi told Tagore that his fight was of a different kind. Tagore replied, "Look down there see what your so-called non-violent followers are up to. They have stolen those pieces of cloth from the bazaar. They have now gone and lit a bonfire with them in my courtyard. You can see for yourself. There they are howling around it like a lot of demented dervishes. Is that non-violence, Gandhiji? Do you think you can hold our violent emotions under firm control with your non-violent principles? You know you can't."

Tagore said, "It hurts me deeply when the cry of rejection rings loud against the West with the clamour that the Western education can only injure us. It can't be true." He was a visionary, far ahead of his times. "We are beginning to discover that our problem is worldwide and no one people of the earth can work out its salvation by detaching itself from the others. Either we shall be saved together or drawn together into destruction." So prophetic. How do you fight a pandemic, or climate change otherwise?

Tagore felt that internationalism is the spirit of the new age. He thought that there is a higher consciousness evolving, a higher mind taking shape. "Any nation which takes an isolated view of its own country will run counter to the spirit of the New Age and knows no peace." He couldn't see any of this spirit in India, but he could see it in the West, he saw there "a real anxiety and effort of their higher mind to rise superior to business considerations." In the West, he could see individuals imbued "with the true spirit of the sannyasin renouncing their home-world in order to achieve the unity of man, by destroying the bondage of nationalism; men who have within their own soul have realised the Advaita of humanity." Advaita of humanity means the oneness of humanity.

India cannot isolate itself from this new world by being "content with telling the beads of negation, harping on others' faults and proceeding with the erosion of swaraj on a foundation of quarrelsomeness." Nationalism to Tagore is an erosion of swaraj, which is a little ironic but still very true.

But Gandhi did not agree. Gandhi's argument was Indian nationalism "is not exclusive, nor aggressive, nor destructive. It is health-giving, religious and therefore humanitarian." The question is, is that indeed so?

I don't think Indian nationalism turned out to be how Gandhi was describing it. Indian textbooks promoted an anti-British sentiment. They did not promote any sense of gratitude, any sense of thankfulness to the British, or to the larger world which was involved in the creation of the modern civilisation. The books failed to teach that sense of unity of humankind.

Think on it

1. How did the global developments impact Tagore's views on nationalism?
2. Why was internationalism important to Tagore?
3. Is internationalism an emerging phenomenon in our times?
4. What is your view on the nature of Indian nationalism?

CHAPTER TWELVE

As Gandhi's Conscience

Although there is a lot of ideological convergence between Gandhi and Tagore, there are certain distinct personality differences between the two. Gandhi is more duty-oriented, with a deep sense of discipline and morality, whereas Tagore is more freedom-loving and creative, with a free mind that is capable of a more direct perception of truth. Tagore is more feeling-oriented and less thought-oriented. After going through many conversations between them, I think that Tagore represents a more evolved consciousness than Gandhi. I feel it so strongly that I dare say Gandhi would need many more cycles of birth and rebirth to reach the level of Tagore.

[1]

Sometimes disagreements happened between Tagore and Gandhi on certain things. Once when Gandhi visited Santiniketan, for instance, he found that the upper-caste students were sitting in a separate place from the lower-caste students. Gandhi wanted all the students to sit together. But Tagore did not agree, saying that anything forced would not be permanent. Tagore too of course wanted the same thing as Gandhi, but he wanted the students themselves to realise it, otherwise what is the point of education?

[2]

Once some boys from South Africa who were trained under Gandhi came to visit Santiniketan. Tagore made this observation about them. "They are trained to obey, which is bad for a human being. These boys are in danger of forgetting to wish for anything and wishing is the best part of attainment." Gandhi believed in discipline, and Tagore believed in a free spirit.

Education should foster freedom of mind and spirit, and not just burden students with information. Tagore said, "From our childhood habits are formed and knowledge is imparted in such a manner that our life is weaned away from nature and our mind and the world are set in opposition from the beginning of our days. We are made to lose our world to find a bagful of information instead. We rob the child of his earth to teach him geography, of language to teach him grammar."

[3]

Take their views on Hindu-Muslim unity. This conversation took place around the time of the non-cooperation movement when Gandhi came to Santiniketan. Gandhi simply said to Tagore, "Gurudev, I have already achieved Hindu-Muslim unity." Gandhi was referring to how the Muslims were brought on the issue of Khilafat during the non-cooperation movement.

But Tagore could see that it would be very fleeting. He said, "I do not agree. You have persuaded Muslims and Hindus to sit side by side on the political platform and to crack a whip together at the British Raj. How far down in their hearts and minds does this sense of unity you talk about penetrate within the minds of your Muslim and Hindu followers? When the British either walk out or are driven out, will Hindus and Muslims then lie down peacefully together? You know they will not!"

As we know, Hindu-Muslim conflict would rage. But what is Tagore's solution to it? Tagore said to Gandhi, "Only when the children of our different religions, communities and castes have been schooled together can you hope to overcome the violent feelings which exist today between Hindu and Muslim, between high caste and low caste."

When Gandhi replied that he too believed in the role of education, Tagore again disagreed, saying, "You first pick out the brightest of the young men and enlist them in your political organisation. The less bright you allow to open schools that can offer only a travesty of education." Tagore was saying that to Gandhi politics came much before education.

[4]

Tagore did not like Gandhi's obsession with the charkha. He said, "Only one means of attaining swaraj has been definitely ordered and the rest is vast silence." He said that Gandhi restricted his approach "to one narrow field alone." Tagore derided the philosophy of charkha, saying, "Spin and weave, spin and weave. How can swaraj be brought about by everyone engaging for a time in spinning?"

Tagore said he is simply not able to obey the call "to burn foreign clothes." He once said that he considered it his first duty "to put up a valiant fight against this terrible habit of blindly obeying orders." Tagore was not saying that the charkha was wrong, but he was questioning its imposition and Gandhi's obsession with it.

[5]

Once Gandhi was trying to enlist Tagore's participation in the non-cooperation movement. During that conversation, Tagore asks Gandhi a very interesting question. "Gandhiji, why do you allow your followers to call you a Mahatma? Are you a Mahatma?" Gandhi replies, "Of course, I am not. But Indians by nature have always been worshippers of symbols, of images. They need an image. If they take me for one, will that not help them to mobilise and to suffer for such a noble cause?" Tagore says, "I wonder whether you are being quite fair to our people, or honest with them." Though the title of Mahatma was given to Gandhi only by Tagore.

[6]

On the matter of idolatry in Hinduism, once Gandhi is reported to have said to Tagore, "That painted piece of stone is the only tangible symbol of God our half-starved brother has ever had. How can we deny him the only link between himself and God?" Gandhi was saying, we may not believe in the worship of idols, but it may be a good thing for many others, especially the poor and lower-caste people seeking help from God. But Tagore did not agree. He said, "If beads and painted stones are not right for us, then they are not right for any of our people, however lowly."

[7]

Tagore disagreed with Gandhi on the validity of the caste system. Gandhi said the vocational division is fine, to which Tagore replied that vocational divisions when perpetuated, lead to anything else but sterility in the long run. Tagore said making vocation depend on birth is simply unscientific.

We can see that Tagore was so clear-thinking while Gandhi was still stuck in the traditions and prejudices of the past.

[8]

On Jan 15, 1934, an earthquake ravaged Bihar. Gandhi said, "Earthquake is a divine chastisement for the great sin we have committed and are still committing against those whom we describe as untouchables."

Condemning Gandhi, Tagore wrote, "This kind of unscientific view of things are too readily accepted by a large section of our countrymen."

Interestingly, Gandhi did not say sorry, he only said that he said what he believed in. He explained his logic, saying "I have long believed that physical phenomena produce both physical and spiritual. The converse I hold to be equally true." Spiritual phenomena will produce physical phenomena. He goes on to say that in this case, "the connection is instinctively felt by me."

Why mutual bonding

Despite their differences, Tagore and Gandhi were very close to each other. Before Gandhi started his fasting against the communal award in 1932, he wrote to Tagore, "If your heart approves of the action I want your blessing." Tagore replied, "Our sorrowing hearts will follow your sublime penance with reverence and love."

I think Gandhi always saw a higher version of himself in Tagore, though they sometimes had arguments. In 1945, Gandhi revealed how Tagore and he were of one mind, saying, "I started with a disposition to detect a conflict between Gurudev and myself but ended with the glorious discovery that there was none."

Tagore felt a similar closeness with Gandhi. In July 1939, just before his death, Tagore made it clear why he admired Gandhi so much, saying, "Though I have the imagination to conceive, I have not the power to carry out. Only few men in the world have this power. And since our country has had the good fortune of giving birth to such a man, the way should be kept clear for his progress – I certainly would never think of impeding it." Gandhi was a man of action. Tagore too tried to get into social activism, but he couldn't pursue it. For Tagore, some important part of him was being realised through Gandhi.

Think on it

1. What was the emphasis of Gandhi on education?
2. What was the emphasis of Tagore in education?
3. What were Tagore's views on Gandhi's concept of charkha?
4. What were Tagore's views on Hindu-Muslim unity?
5. What were Tagore's views on the validity of the caste system?
6. Why did Gandhi feel a bonding with Tagore?
7. Why did Tagore admire Gandhi?

Sri Aurobindo

More a Scholar Than a Yogi

Sri Aurobindo (1872–1950) is regarded as an accomplished yogi. In his youth, he was involved in fighting for India's freedom for some years, but he quit politics and dedicated himself wholly to spiritual pursuits. He moved to Pondicherry from Calcutta, set up an ashram and became a prolific writer. Aurobindo lived in England for many years as a student, right from the age of 7. Back in India, he worked in the service of the princely state of Baroda for a few years, then he worked as a teacher at a college in Baroda. He had been taking increasingly more interest in the politics of the Indian independence movement. Later he worked as the principal of the National College at Calcutta.

Aurobindo was popular as a leader of extremists, along with Bipin Chandra Pal and Lala Lajpat Roy. For his alleged role in the Alipore bomb conspiracy, which was about an assassination attempt made on a district judge in 1908, he had to spend a year in the Alipore jail. During his stay in the jail, he had a mystical experience that transformed him. He realised his mission was not in politics but spirituality. He moved to Pondicherry, which was then under French control. Pursuing the path of spirituality, he would go on to write some major works such as The Life Divine, The Synthesis of Yoga, and The Ideal of Human Unity.

Nationalism is God's work

Although Aurobindo gave up politics, he continued to write extensively on things related to India's freedom and nationhood, placing them in a more spiritual context. Aurobindo's ideas on nationalism are part of his ideas on the nature of human existence. He believed that Indian freedom was God's work. According to Aurobindo, God was cooperating with India in getting freedom. One may think what is this, how can God be interested in such a thing. One has to understand that Aurobindo's God is not like the common man's God, such as Lord Venkateshwara, to whom one can pray and have one's wish granted. To Aurobindo, God is like one divine source or a higher source. You can also call it Spirit. This God is Spirit or the divine source of all life, and it is ensuring that life on Earth is evolving in a particular direction. India's freedom is but a part of this general evolution of humanity.

This is similar to Hegel's idea on Spirit. It is the Spirit that impels life on Earth to evolve in the direction of greater freedom. This greater freedom can be achieved when all humanity becomes one. This is part of the design of God or Spirit. Aurobindo says, "The unity of mankind is evidently a part of Nature's eventual scheme and must come about." This is also just the way Hegel thought.

Teilhard de Chardin was another twentieth-century philosopher who also believed in the Spirit-driven inevitability of human evolution. Aurobindo says, "Indeed, it is God's will that we should be ourselves, we should recognise ourselves" (The Ideal of Karma Yogin). When we get to know ourselves, we become spiritually realised and free. But if it is God's wish that India should be free, then why would he have made India face the repression of the British in the first place? To Aurobindo, all that suffering is a part of the growing process. He says, "Repression is nothing but the hammer of God that is beating us into shape so that we may be moulded into a mighty nation and an instrument for his work in the world" (The Human Cycle). This is reminiscent of Nietzsche's idea that through suffering one becomes mighty.

India's role

When God is guiding India, what is He expecting from the people of the country? Aurobindo has some deeper ideas about what is India, what is its destiny, and what is its role in shaping the future of mankind. Aurobindo thinks that every country has something to offer. Different countries have different cultures, and different capabilities and each has to make some unique contribution to God's work. Aurobindo thinks India's uniqueness lies in its spirituality.

Aurobindo first wants India to become a stronger nation. India was not yet a clear-cut nation-state in the early decades of the twentieth century. Its national identity was just emerging. India had been a nation "only in the sense of having a common soul-life, a common culture, a common social organisation, a common political head, but not a nation-state" (The Human Cycle). The emergence of a sense of national identity was impeded for centuries because India was divided into self-sufficient villages which were like little republics. Aurobindo wants the relative isolation and independence of these villages to be a thing of the past. He says, "The day of the independent village or group of villages has gone and must not be revived."

We have to decisively move towards a future of strong, independent nationhood. All the villages, towns, cities and regions of India should come together as one nation. "The nation demands its hour of fulfilment and seeks to gather the village life of its rural population into a mighty single and compact democratic nationality. We must make the nation what the village community was of old, self-sufficient, self-centred, autonomous and exclusive – the ideal of national swaraj"

This new India should give the gift of yoga to the larger world. In general parlance, yoga means a set of physical exercises but that's a very narrow connotation. In spirituality, yoga means any great striving to merge with the Spirit. Aurobindo wants a spiritual revolution to happen in the world, and India would lead the way. He says, "We believe that it is to make yoga the ideal of human life that India rises today. By the yoga, she will get the strength to realise her freedom, unity and greatness, by yoga she will keep the strength to preserve it. It is a spiritual revolution we foresee and the material is only shadow or reflex" (The Ideal).

India will progress materially and economically too, but that would be secondary, India's primary focus would be its spirituality. India will rise, but not by imitating the more developed nations of the West, it will rise in its own way. "The nineteenth century in India was imitative, self-forgetful, artificial. It aimed at successful reproduction of Europe in India, forgetting the deep saying of Gita, 'Better the law of one's own being though it be badly done than an alien dharma well followed; death in one's own dharma is better, it is a dangerous thing to follow the law of another's nature.' For death in one's own dharma brings new birth, success in an alien path means only successful suicide" (The Ideal of Karmayogin).

We have to embrace our Indianness. But that doesn't mean we accept all that is evil in our culture too. "We must revolt not only against tendency towards Europeanisation but also against everything bad in India. This has been the spirit of Hinduism in the past, and there is no reason why it should be different." Change is essential, but this change will not destroy our soul, it will only help us express our soul better. He says, "We will sacrifice no ancient form to an unreasoning love of change, we will keep none which the national spirit deserves to replace by one that is still a better and truer expression of the undying soul of the nation" (The Ideal).

The idea of freedom

What kind of political and economic system Aurobindo might prefer? Aurobindo is very clear that he is not for capitalism which is an expression of materialism. Nor is he for something like socialism or communism, where there is no more liberty. Aurobindo has a particular notion of freedom, and that freedom wouldn't exist in materialist capitalism or oppressive socialism.

Freedom is not simply a freedom to consume anything, freedom to buy anything. "It is a spiritual, an inner freedom that alone can create a perfect human order." "A large liberty will be the law of a spiritual society and the increase in freedom a sign of the growth of human society towards the possibility of true spiritualisation." Free individuals "would not feel themselves complete except in the free growth of others."

The individual cannot flourish without society, nor the society can grow crushing the individual. "Every time the society crushes or effects the individual, it is inflicting a wound on itself and depriving its own life of a priceless source of stimulation and growth. The individual too cannot flourish by himself, for the universal, the unity and the collectivity of his fellow beings, is his present source of stock" (The Human Cycle).

Evaluation

In summary, Aurobindo says India should be independent, and its role is to contribute to the spirituality of mankind. India has something great to do, so even God would help in making it free. This is no different from some others who would say why India should be powerful and wealthy. Aurobindo's nationalism is called spiritual nationalism. But I do not see any spirituality in this.

Aurobindo fails to see the problem with a growing sense of nationalism. A lot of violence in post-independent India was based on the idea of nationalism. We took the flag so seriously that many atrocities were committed by the Indian state in its name. We were willing to take away others' freedom in the name of nationalism. Aurobindo, who was predicting the evolution of higher consciousness towards greater freedom and human unity failed to see the immediate problems coming from nationalism.

More importantly, what is the spirituality that India has to contribute? I'd say that Indian spirituality is about the self. How the self is constructed, its illusory nature, and how the self is responsible for other problems. A person like Aurobindo who knows this should explain how the identity of a nation also creates problems. How a nation works against human unity should be emphasised. How a nation can work against its own people can be explained.

The kind of nation he envisaged was a kind of ego enlargement of a group. It is simple ego aggrandisement. It appears that Aurobindo spoke, at least in the context of nationalism, more like a scholar than a yogi. Rabindranath Tagore did a much more sensible job of explaining to the people the evils and problems of nationalism, which Aurobindo, an adept in spirituality, should have done to a greater extent but did not at all.

Think on it

1. Why did Aurobindo go to Pondicherry?
2. What was Aurobindo's notion of Spirit?
3. In which direction is humanity evolving?
4. What is India's role in the context of the larger world?
5. Why was India not a nation-state before the British?
6. What is Aurobindo's idea of human freedom?
7. Why did Aurobindo oppose both capitalism and socialism?
8. Did Aurobindo discuss the problems associated with taking nationalism seriously?

M N Roy

CHAPTER FOURTEEN

A Marxist View of Freedom Struggle

Manabendra Nath Roy (1887–1954) is a noted Marxist thinker, who started with a brief stint as a terrorist in India's freedom struggle. In the later years of his life, he went on to evolve his humanistic philosophy. His thinking went through some fundamental ideological shifts from time to time.

M N Roy was a Bengali Brahmin, who was at first influenced by the terrorist philosophy and believed in the use of violence to trouble the British. When the British were trying to catch him, he escaped to the US where he was influenced by socialism. From there, he went to Mexico where he was involved in the formation of the Mexican communist party. As a communist party member, he went to Moscow to take part in the second congress of Communist International in 1920. There he offered critical comments on Lenin's Draft Thesis on the National and Colonial Question. His views made him famous in the communist party circles. He was liked by Lenin, and later even by Stalin. In 1927, he headed a delegation of Communist International to China to guide the movement there.

But Roy then fell out with Stalin and was expelled from the Comintern. He returned to India in 1930. For his subversive activities earlier, the British government jailed him for six years.

He was with Congress from 1930 to 1940, and then he founded Radical Democratic Party, which was dissolved in 1948. He then lost belief in party politics and developed a new ideology called radical humanism.

The colonial question

As used by the communists, 'the colonial question' is a phrase that referred to formulating a stand for the communists on the issue of colonialism and the nationalist movements going on in the colonies. What should a communist make of a nationalist movement like the one led by Gandhi? The communists looked at society mostly in terms of class struggle, they did not believe that a nation was an important identity.

Lenin believed that the downfall of both capitalism and imperialism could take place through the colonies. The anti-colonial struggle was discussed in terms of classes in communist circles. As Lenin saw it, the anti-colonial movement in many colonies was led by the colonial bourgeoisie, because they were discriminated against by the imperial bourgeoisie. The native bourgeoisie wanted to include other classes and launch a common struggle against colonialism. The upper classes were mobilising the lower classes in the name of nationalism. However, these upper classes wouldn't want socialism, they would want to retain the old structure but with themselves as the rulers.

In this kind of situation, what did the communist parties have to do? That was Lenin's question. He answered that the communist parties should side with the nationalist bourgeoisie but only temporarily. After gaining freedom, the communist party should work to bring about socialism, whereas the bourgeoisie would want to establish a parliamentary democracy.

M N Roy's thesis

M N Roy differed from Lenin when he presented his thesis at the second congress of the Communist International. Roy felt that the bourgeois leadership in the anti-colonial struggle wouldn't survive for long. As the anti-colonial struggle becomes more radicalised, the bourgeois leadership will be eliminated. From then on, the communist party should lead the freedom struggle. Roy felt that Lenin's position if accepted, meant a once-for-all acceptance of a subordinate position for the communist parties.

So Roy thought in 1920 that Congress would lose its leadership position soon. As the elements of militancy come to dominate the freedom struggle, the bourgeois leadership would be thrown into the dustbin of history. Only the communists would lead a country to the final victory. The nationalist revolution should be indistinguishable from the socialist revolution and be led by a proletarian party. Thus, Roy gave more importance to communist parties and immediate role to them. His thesis was also adopted in the second congress. Roy would be entrusted with the leadership of the communists in India.

On Gandhian struggle

M N Roy initially liked Gandhi's concept of the non-cooperation movement, he praised Gandhi, he said that through the non-cooperation movement "the agrarian movement, the proletarian movement and the nationalist movement are moving concertedly towards one object, national independence." Roy said that Gandhi was trying "to break the class insularity of the Congress and to make it truly representative of the national aspirations of all classes of Indians." He also said that the non-cooperation movement was "much more dangerous than an armed uprising, which can always be met face to face and put down." Roy asserted that it was "the only path" against the repressive colonial government.

But by the early 20s M N Roy became very critical of the non-cooperation movement, he said that it has failed. Roy had always been critical of the Gandhian ideal of development and his ideas on technology. Once, criticising Gandhi's obsession with the charkha, Roy said that the charkha has already been "relegated to its well-deserved place in the museum." Roy became a full-blown critic of Gandhian philosophy. "Gandhism is the acutest and most desperate manifestation of the forces of reaction trying to hold their own against the objectively revolutionary tendencies contained in the liberal-bourgeois nationalism. The impending wane of Gandhism signifies the collapse of the reactionary forces and their total elimination from the political movement."

In 1924 when the Swarajists won some elections to the councils, M N Roy was elated and said that "the defeat of orthodox Gandhism is complete and final; the Swarajists have won the day and Mr Gandhi, as leader of the Indian national struggle, has sung his swansong." Roy thought that Gandhi failed because of some inherent contradictions in his philosophy. Gandhi's undoing lies in his "obstinate and futile desire to unite all the Indian people, landlords and peasants, capitalists and proletariat, moderates and extremists, in a common struggle for an undefined goal."

Roy viewed India's freedom struggle exclusively as a class struggle. "The movement for national liberation is a struggle of the native middle class against the economic and political monopoly of the imperialist bourgeoisie." The freedom struggle will become less and less of one country clashing with another and more and more of a direct class struggle of working people against all exploiters. "When the working class will begin the struggle earnestly, it is expected to be more of a social nature than a political movement for national liberation. Since 1918, the Indian movement has entered this stage. It may still have an appearance of a national struggle involving the mass of the population, but fundamentally it is social strife, the revolt of the exploited against the exploiting class, irrespective of nationality."

India In transition

M N Roy wrote a book on Indian polity and economy in 1922, titled 'India in Transition '. This was the first systematic exposition of the Marxist view of Indian history.

M N Roy followed the method Marx used to understand 19th century Europe. Marx identified four classes: bourgeoisie, petty bourgeoisie, peasantry and proletariat. In the Indian context, Roy made a different classification, there were the landed aristocracy, the bourgeoisie, the intellectuals, the petty peasantry, and the working class (including the landless peasants). The bourgeoisie in India was a product of colonialism. What did they want? They may seem to be fighting for national liberation, but it may not be what they want. They would agree to a subordinate role and be willing to make a compromise with the imperialists. What M N Roy proposed in his alternative thesis to the colonial question at the second congress of the Comintern was given a detailed treatment in this book.

Think on it

1. How did M N Roy come to participate in the second congress of Communist International?
2. What was Lenin's idea on the role of the communist parties in the anti-colonial struggle?
3. What was Roy's idea on the role of the communist party in the Indian anti-colonial struggle?
4. Why did M N Roy see the Gandhian approach as a failure?
5. Was M N Roy's understanding of the Gandhian struggle right?

CHAPTER FIFTEEN

Radical Humanism Is Impractical

After M N Roy moved away from Marxism, he proposed what he called new humanism or radical humanism. Humanism refers to keeping human beings as the central entity for whose wellbeing any system is created. Man is the end. One may think, are there any systems where man is not the end? Indeed there are certain systems which are making a man an instrument of something bigger than him. For instance, take the idea of a nation. If an individual is asked to make some sacrifice for the sake of a nation, then man is not at the centre. Roy rejected nationalism, which was rejected by Marxists too.

However, in the place of the nation, Marxists proposed the concept of class solidarity. They glorified class struggle, they thought of the society in terms of classes, and ultimately the proletarian class was expected to establish communism. For that, there needs to be a communist party. This party was made the centre and not man. Roy had firsthand experience of how things could go wrong in socialism because he worked for Stalin and saw what he was doing.

Man is to be the sovereign. Society or a nation is to help man to be free. Roy felt that the essence of a human being is his search for freedom. That freedom called for one to have a sense of control over one's life and a confidence that one can shape one's destiny using mind and reason. It is also about having certain values, a moral code. Within the bounds of ethics and rationality, an individual is supposed to pursue freedom. The purpose of education is to create such men and women.

During his Marxist phase, M N Roy had rejected parliamentary democracy on the ground that it was empowering only a few rich people. When M N Roy was disillusioned with Marxism, he didn't change his views on parliamentary democracy.

Roy disagreed with Marx himself. He said Marx's concept of materialism is not true. "I categorically reject the view that ethical values, cultural patterns, movements of ideas, are mere ideological super-structures raised to justify established economic relations." Nor should history be explained in terms of dialectical materialism. He says that history must be studied as the process of "integral human evolution – mental, intellectual, social." Ideas play an important role. Man can think and should think and shape history rather than assume that he is simply subjected to certain inexorable historical laws.

M N Roy rejected Lenin's glorification of the party system. Roy says, "As power is never voluntarily abdicated, freedom for all is impossible. The collective ego – nation, class – is invented to justify the perpetual slavery of the majority." He says, "The individuality of its members was sacrificed at the altar of the collective ego of the party and a party is the archetype of the society it proposes to build." He says, "Delegation of power to a small minority means abdication of power as had happened in Russia. In the name of the class or the nation, the party became a new ruler, the proletarian state became its vested interest."

Roy proposes thinking in terms of individual welfare. "Political thinking had emphasised the state. The social welfare was considered as something bigger than mere sum total of the welfare, no progress or prosperity can be actually experienced except by individuals." He says, "No freedom, no welfare, no progress or prosperity can be actually experienced except by individuals." He says, "Individual is prior to the society. Society is the means for attaining an end, which is freedom and progress of the individual"

Village republics

Roy says "Freedom is the supreme value because the urge for freedom is the essence of human existence." If a man should be at the centre, then he should be part of smaller political structures over which he can have control.

Roy thought of his ideal polity in terms of local republics, like Indian villages. If a political system is of small scale then direct democracy is possible, and then democracy can be participatory. There will be many republics, and they will constitute the entire society, and the state would be far less significant than it is now. There is not much for the state to do or deliver in Roy's political system.

The concept of a reduced role for the state or its total disappearance is there in Marxism and Gandhism too. While Marx came to this position through communism, Gandhi came to it through his emphasis on village republics. Gandhi's ideas and M N Roy's ideas are more or less the same, though Roy was critical of everything about Gandhi including the ideology of non-violence which Roy thought was used to prevent the movement from turning radical.

Roy says about local republics, "The state will not then be able to become an all-powerful Leviathan, because state power will be decentralised, being largely vested in the local republics. In other words, the state will in this way become coterminous with society"

"Then the time will come when a centralised Leviathan can no longer pose as democracy, but a democratic state composed of a number of local democratic republics will rise in which direct democracy is a reality. It will come into being not by passing of laws, not by imposition from above, but because local democracies will be in existence as a political reality and give the impress of their structure on the state as a whole"

The problem with a weak state

However, there is a fundamental problem with the idea of having no state or a weak state. In one society you have village republics and a weak state, and then nearby there is a strong state. This strong state will attack the weak state and conquer it, so how could a weak state survive? Many stateless societies were subordinated this way by the state.

When you think of a political entity, you have to think in terms of its security first. One can argue if every state is weak as the other, then the security problem would not be there, but how can one be sure of that? Wherever there is a strong state, it can invade all the weak states with small communities and enslave them.

Historically that is how states emerged, they did not emerge because people wanted to live together, they emerged as a way for people living in many communities to secure protection from external threats.

You do need a strong state. You do need a large political polity. You need to work out the relationship between the large entity and the small communities like village republics. What kind of a political system will this large entity follow? Will it be socialist? Will it be a parliamentary democracy? We are back to the same set of questions.

In the context of India, things get even worse because of deep-rooted caste system and other evils in our villages. If these villages are given the freedom to rule themselves, then exploitation would run rampant. The so-called radical humanism fails to answer any of the big social and political questions.

Dreamy thinking

M N Roy says that in an ideal system, "there will be no contradiction between collective responsibility and individual liberty. Social obligations will be voluntarily undertaken and discharged, in quest of individual freedom, by upholding his or her potentialities, that is to say, by asserting individuality, each society will increase his social utility and thus contribute to the sum total of collective well-being and progress" How would this be possible? This might remind one of Marx's statement: From each according to one's capacity, to each according to one's need.

Roy says, "New Humanism is cosmopolitan. A cosmopolitan commonwealth of spiritually free men will not be limited by the boundaries of national states – capitalist, fascist, socialist, communist, or of any other kind – which will gradually disappear under the impact of the 20th century renaissance of Man." He says, "Radicalism thinks neither in terms of nation, nor class; its concern is man; it conceives freedom as freedom of the individual." How would it be possible?

In my judgement, there is nothing radical about this kind of humanism. You know, in Telugu films one hero is called rebel star, another hero is called power star, and another one is called super star, so just like that somebody's nationalism is called spiritual nationalism though there is nothing much spiritual about it, and M N Roy's philosophy is called radical humanism though there is nothing radical in it. They just give some fancy names to their hazy views. Even if they don't give such names themselves, others give them those.

Man needs small entities as well as big entities. He needs villages as well as nations. Parties are also needed for the functioning of democracy. But it is important to know what is the place of all these bigger entities in the overall well-being of man and not glorify them at the expense of man.

Think on it

1. What is meant by humanism?
2. To what extent did Roy disagree with Marx?
3. Where did Roy disagree with Lenin?

4. What should be the highest value for man, according to Roy?
5. Why did Roy favour village republics?
6. What is the problem if a society has a state that is too weak?
7. What is your overall assessment of Roy's humanism?

Mohammed Iqbal

CHAPTER SIXTEEN

As the Spiritual Father of Pakistan

Mohammed Iqbal (1877–1938) is regarded as an influential Islamic thinker. He is also called Allama Iqbal. Allama means learned. He was born in Sialkot, now in Pakistan. His grandfather was a Kashmiri Brahmin. Iqbal regarded himself as "a son of Kashmiri Brahmins but acquainted with the wisdom of Rumi and Tabriz." Rumi and Tabriz were renowned Sufi saints.

Iqbal worked as a lecturer at Oriental College, Lahore. After that, he left for higher studies first to England and then to Munich where he did his Ph.D., on The Development of Metaphysics in Persia. He returned to India in 1908. From then on he began to reflect on religious issues. He was one of the founding fathers of Jamia Millia Islamia, established at Aligarh in 1920. Gandhi asked him to be its vice-chancellor, but he refused. He was elected to Punjab Legislative Council in 1927.

Iqbal presided over the All India Muslim League in 1930. As the Muslim League's president, he advocated two separate administrative areas in India, one for Hindus and another for Muslims. He attended 2nd and 3rd Round Table Conferences held in London. He is one of the three most important people who contributed to the creation of Pakistan – the other two are Syed Ahmad Khan and Jinnah.

Through his poetry, Iqbal impacted the entire Muslim world. He wrote in Urdu and Persian. He was named the national poet in Pakistan. The Urdu world is familiar with him as the "Poet of the East." In Iran, he is highly regarded for his Persian works. Of his 12,000 verses of poetry, 7000 were in Persian and the remaining were in Urdu. In 1915, his book Secrets of the Self, written in Persian, became very popular. Iqbal's poetry was read and quoted during the 1979 revolution in Iran. His poetry was translated into many European languages.

Ayatollah Ali Khamenei, who is the second supreme leader of Iran and currently the most important person in Iran said on Iqbal: "Iqbal was not acquainted with Persian idiom, as he spoke Urdu at home and talked to his friends in Urdu or English. He did not know the rules of Persian prose writing. In spite of not having tasted the Persian way of life, never living in the cradle of Persian culture, and never having any direct association with it, he cast with great mastery the most delicate, the most subtle and radically new philosophical themes into the mould of Persian poetry, some of which are unsurpassable yet." In the First Iqbal Summit in Tehran in 1986, Khamenei stated about Iran that in its "conviction that the Quran and Islam are to be made the basis of all revolutions and movements, Iran was exactly following the path that was shown to us by Iqbal."

Response to colonialism

Before discussing Iqbal's ideas, let's look at how intellectuals of Asia were responding to colonialism. The British came to India and they started ruling the country. They were also seen as Christians. The intellectuals in India belonged to two different religious communities, Hindu and Muslim.

Some of them thought on the following lines. The West is good but not perfect, and we were good at one time, but now we are poor. We will reform, and we will reclaim our place. This meant learning something from the West, but at the same time, the East also had something to give to the West. Gandhi and Tagore come under this category, and Iqbal too comes under this category, though they may differ on what they regard as bad and good in the East and what to reform.

Like Gandhi, Iqbal was critical of the West. Addressing the students at Cambridge in 1931 Iqbal said: "I would like to offer a few pieces of advice to the young men who are at present studying at Cambridge. I advise you against atheism and materialism. The biggest blunder made by Europe was the separation of Church and State. This deprived their culture of moral soul and diverted it to atheistic materialism. I had 25 years ago seen through the drawbacks of this civilisation and, therefore, had made some prophecies. They had been delivered by my tongue, although I did not quite understand them. This happened in 1907. After six or seven years, my prophecies came true, word by word. The European war of 1914 was an outcome of the mistakes mentioned above made by the European nations in the separation of the Church and the State." To Iqbal, The Frist World War happened because Europe separated religion from politics.

Iqbal was similar to Gandhi in giving a role to religion in politics. Whereas Gandhi believed that every religion contained truth, Iqbal was particular about following Islam. Iqbal says, "My real purpose is to look for a better social order and to present a universally acceptable ideal before the world, but it is impossible for me, in this effort, to outline this ideal, to ignore the social system and values of Islam whose most important objective is to demolish all the artificial and pernicious distinctions of caste, creed, colour and economic status." Iqbal wanted to propose a universally acceptable ideal, and he said how can that ideal not be Islam?

Like Tagore, Iqbal was also critical of nationalism, though for a different reason. To Iqbal, nationalism could mean moving away from Islam. He wanted Muslims all over the world to belong to a single community. "The construction of polity on national lines is unthinkable to a Muslim."

Iqbal was for an Islam-based political system and so he thought Muslims needed separate political arrangements from those of Hindus. Iqbal's reason for the creation of Pakistan was not simply the fear of Hindu domination, it was much more. That's why he is considered the spiritual father of Pakistan. Pakistan was needed not only for the security and protection of the Muslims but also for more positive reasons.

Iqbal said in his 1930 presidential address to the Muslim League, "I would like to see Punjab, the North-West Frontier Province, Sind and Baluchistan amalgamated into a single state. Self-government within the British Empire or without the British Empire, the formation of a consolidated North-West Indian Muslim State appears to me to be the final destiny of the Muslims, at least of North-West India." Note that East Bengal was not included in Iqbal's list. He proposed only a separate administrative arrangement, but this was one of the landmark developments in the creation of Pakistan. He stuck to this stand in the Round Table Conferences. Iqbal feared that otherwise, the Hindu majority would force out Muslim heritage, culture and political influence. Though at one time he wrote poems in praise of Hindustan, saying, "Sare jahan se achcha Hindustan hamara" (India is the best in the whole world) – which is a line he wrote in 1904 – he changed his position completely in the years that followed.

Think on it

1. What is the importance of the Muslim League session of 1930?
2. What do you know about Iqbal as a poet?
3. Why was Iqbal popular in Iran?
4. Why was Iqbal against atheism?
5. Was Iqbal for socialism?
6. Why was Iqbal against secularism?
7. Why was Iqbal against nationalism?

8. Where did Iqbal differ from Gandhi and Tagore? On what would he agree?
9. Why did Iqbal want a separate political entity for Muslims?

Man as God's Agent and Not as a Sufi

Nietzsche impacted Iqbal so much that Iqbal started looking at Islam from the point of view of Nietzsche's philosophy. But he did not take all of Nietzsche's philosophy. Borrowing some insights from Nietzsche, Iqbal developed certain views regarding what caused the decline of the Islamic world.

First, let's look at what Nietzsche's philosophy is and where Iqbal disagreed with him. Nietzsche's philosophy is based on his understanding of Darwinism. He thought of Darwinism as the survival of the strong. This strength is manifested as the will to power, desire to achieve things, and readiness to fight. Nietzsche was against compassion, kindness, and weakness.

Because Christianity glorified compassion, Nietzsche was critical of it. Nietzsche thought Christianity taught the wrong values. Interestingly, Nietzsche preferred Islam to Christianity. Nietzsche thought that Islam taught the values that were needed for strength and survival, the masculine qualities.

Nietzsche said about Christianity. "Christianity destroyed for us the whole harvest of ancient civilisation, and later it also destroyed for us the whole harvest of Mohammedan civilisation." Nietzsche was unhappy about this. "There should be no choice in the matter when faced with Islam and Christianity. War to the knife with

Rome! Peace and friendship with Islam." He preferred Islam because it glorified strength and not kindness.

Iqbal reflected on these issues. Nietzsche's superman possessed the qualities Iqbal valued. Iqbal then came up with an ideal of the perfect man, khudi[1] – who is Nietzsche's superman with some modifications. Iqbal didn't agree with everything about Nietzsche. He wanted Nietzsche's glorification of power, strength, and readiness to fight, but Iqbal did not agree with Nietzsche's position that God was dead. Iqbal thought God is very much there. A man also should have god-like qualities, such as kindness and compassion.

'Perfect man' is the English equivalent to what Iqbal called khudi. Iqbal's perfect man has certain god-like attributes, not simply aggressiveness. While Nietzsche's superman may believe only in reason, Iqbal's perfect man believes there are other ways of knowing too, such as intuition and revelation.

After making these modifications to Nietzsche's superman, Iqbal says man should be God's agent on the earth. What is meant by being God's agent on the earth? Most people, including Iqbal, equate God first with power and strength. God has kindness, God is just, God knows everything, and God punishes the unjust. God is not prejudiced. A man should be an agent of such a God. What has this got to do with the contemporary problems that Islam was facing? Why is this issue of the perfect man, khudi, important in the context of Islam?

Iqbal thought that the Muslim world at one time had the perfect man as an ideal, but later a Sufi saint became its ideal. Sufism's goals are losing the ego and merging with God. Loss of ego would mean loss of desire, becoming quiet, happy, and contented. Iqbal thought such religious idealism was the reason for the downfall of Islam. Iqbal's criticism of Islam is the same as Nietzsche's criticism of Christianity.

Iqbal thought that in the beginning, it was the perfect man who was held as an ideal. The prophet was a perfect man as well as a messenger. He was God's agent. He wanted others to emulate him. He didn't want to lose his ego. He was not one with God. These ideals were lost with time and the Muslims started glorifying Sufism. Then the decline of Islam started.

Man is God's vicegerent on the earth. "Man becomes unique by becoming more and more like the most unique individual [God]." "He executes the command of Allah in the world." As God's servant, man wants to establish God's rule on the earth. He works with this end in view.

Iqbal equated inaction with Sufism. "Life is latent in seeking/ Its origin is hidden in desire/ Keep desire alive in thine heart/ Lest thy little dust become a tomb/ Negation of desire is death to living/ Even an absence of heat extinguishes the flame." Sufism taught the doctrine of "oneness of being" (wahdat al-wujud). Its goal is the dissolution of the self (fana), which would imply no concern with action and achievement, as Iqbal saw it.

Man needs to have tension, which a Sufi does not have. Iqbal wrote, "Personality is the state of tension and can continue only if that state is maintained. Since the personality, or the state of tension, is the most valuable achievement of man, he should see that he does not revert to a state of relaxation." He said, "Men of God do not become God/ but they are never separated from God."

Evaluation

What do you make of all this? I can only say that the pleasure of achievement and success involves one kind of fulfilment, but there is a higher kind of meaning unrelated to success and failure. Iqbal failed to see this.

Iqbal wrote, "The mystic does not wish to return from the repose of 'unitary experience'; and even when he does return, as he must, his return does not mean much for mankind at large. The prophet's return is creative. He returns to insert himself into the sweep of time with a view to controlling forces of history, and thereby a fresh world of ideals."

Buddha realised the ultimate truth but he also impacted the world profoundly. Many Sufi saints too had a great impact on the world. The way the prophet impacted the world is of one kind, the way the Sufis impacted the world is of another kind. To Iqbal, impacting the world meant establishing empires. He did not see that an impact can be made on people to help them live happily and wisely.

On Sufi saints

Iqbal's views on certain Sufi saints bring more clarity on his philosophy. Mansur al-Hallaj (858–922) is known for his proclamation of "Ana al-Haqq," "I am the Truth." It was considered blasphemy and he was persecuted. Iqbal believed Mansur al-Hallaj's statement was misinterpreted. "The true interpretation is not the drop slipping into the ocean, but the realisation and bold affirmation in an undying phrase of the reality and permanence of the human ego in a profounder personality." To Iqbal, this controversial statement meant having a perfect ego, not the dropping of ego.

Iqbal thought this entire thing about ego dissolution came from the school of Ibn Arabi (1165–1240). It was basically from the 13th century onwards. Iqbal liked Rumi (1207–73) very much but not Hafiz (1325–89). Iqbal found the Sufism of Rumi was active but that of Hafiz was inactive. Iqbal took Rumi as his spiritual guide, whereas he had an intense dislike of Hafiz. Incidentally, Tagore is said to have been very much impacted by Hafiz's philosophy.

Iqbal wrote on Hafiz:

"Beware of Hafiz, the drinker

His cup is full of the poison of death.

He is a Muslim, but his belief wears the thread of an unbeliever.

His proposition Is nothing but hearsay.

He is a sheep and yet has learnt to sing.

His fascination is a poison, that is all,

He gives weakness the name of strength,

His music leads the nation astray,
His congregation is not for the pious;
His cup is not for the ingenious ones,
Beware of Hafiz, and do not be sheep."

What Iqbal wrote here became very controversial and finally, this poem was dropped from his book Secrets of the Self.But that didn't mean Iqbal changed his opinion. This poem might clarify the point Iqbal was very particular about. We should try to understand Iqbal's point instead of simply appreciating his poetry.

Think on it

1. Why was Nietzsche critical of Christianity?
2. Where did Iqbal disagree with Nietzsche?
3. On what did Iqbal agree with Nietzsche?
4. What was the reason for the downfall of Islam as a world religion?
5. What are Iqbal's views on Rumi and Hafiz?

[1] From Reconstructing the Muslim Self: Muhammad Iqbal, Khudi and the Modern Self by Hasan Azad, published in Islamophobia Journal in Fall 2014.

CHAPTER EIGHTEEN

Was Sufism the Cause of Islam's downfall?

The idea that Sufism was responsible for the downfall of Islam is very difficult to accept for me. Sufism, I'd say, is the flowering of Islam. Islam started with a simple moral code. As it arose from a primitive political and economic system, it was legalistic and God-fearing.

Then a group of dedicated Muslims went on setting up empires. They conquered many lands through their motivation and belief in God. They fought with the best of existing civilisations and won, they picked up science, they picked up culture, architecture and philosophy. They added many new concepts to Islam, including religious ones. What started in a primitive society became a worldwide religion through accommodation and absorption of various cultures, and increasing depth over time. If Muslims wanted to impose the Quranic code on everybody, there would have been a lot of resistance.

Iqbal himself belonged to Kashmir where Sufism played a major role in the conversion of the Hindus to Islam. People of other great religions felt connected to Sufism. It was peace-loving and did not glorify aggression. It was a search for inner peace. Why is Sufism popular worldwide even now? Because it has great depth, which provides meaning to life.

What Iqbal was proposing was going back to Islam's roots, which meant he did not know what contributed to the greatness of Islam, he did not know what is great about Islam. Iqbal thought of greatness in terms of military conquest, he did not think in terms of the purpose of religion, which is to foster calmness, inner peace, tolerance, harmony, and happiness.

Rise of the West

Muslims ask what caused Islam's downfall, and Hindus too ask what caused the Hindu downfall. They often miss the point that the cause was not what happened to them but rather what happened elsewhere. The discoveries of new lands, the English Revolution, the Scientific Revolution, the Industrial Revolution, and the Enlightenment – all of them happened in Europe. For a variety of reasons, some countries come up with certain new ideas and if these ideas are powerful enough, they spread across the world. It was just the way Islam also had spread.

Modernisation was a new ideology that was so powerful. Through the power of technology and reason, the Europeans conquered the whole world. The Western civilisation conquered the world in a way that no other previous civilisations could do.

We can't say the Muslims themselves should have evolved such thoughts. Or the Hindus. The Western civilisation too will have some end, just like Islam had its days of glory and Hinduism had its. That's the way nature works.

If the question is why Muslims did not achieve what the West achieved or why the Muslim world lagged, the reason would not be Sufism. The West achieved what it achieved not by pursuing its religion but by moving away from it, towards reason. The West moved forward, creating ideologies that were counter to their traditions and religious values. If Iqbal had any sense of history, he should have said that the decline of the Islamic world was because Muslims were still too tied to Islam and they should move away from it.

Iqbal was critical of Sufism, but not of Islam. He evaluated others in terms of Islam. He said Nietzsche's problem was that he did not believe in God, he said the same thing about Lenin. Iqbal's observation that World War I happened due to secularism is wrong. Being religious would not prevent wars. Allah's agents could fight among themselves calling one's fight a jehad!

To know why Islam declined, and why it continues to have problems even now, we need not go anywhere. Iqbal's unquestioning belief in Islam shows what the problem with Islam is. How distant it is from producing its Galileo, Nietzsche or Bertrand Russell who could write a book like 'Why I am Not a Christian'.

Iqbal's thought stands as proof of how unthinking the Muslim community was then. Tragically, Muslim intellectuals did not change much from his times, though the world they are facing is far more challenging and less conducive to old ways of thought.

Iqbal is regarded as the spiritual founder of Pakistan. What kind of spirituality is he offering to the people of Pakistan? The project of linking the tradition with the present was not wrong – Gandhi too was trying to do that. But what elements of the past you take and what change you want is what matters. Iqbal's effort was not in the wrong direction, but his conclusions were wrong.

Sufism could serve the purpose of taking Muslims forward. It can be a better approach to the problems like fundamentalism and sectarianism – which Iqbal did not even foresee.

Think on it

1. What events contributed to the rise of the West?
2. What was the attitude of the West towards their religion?
3. Is there a need for Muslims to be more critical of their religion?
4. Is Sufism better in creating a better environment for Muslims to grow?

B.R. Ambedkar

CHAPTER NINETEEN

Can Muslims Be Patriotic Under Hindu Rule?

In his book Pakistan or Partition of India (1940), B.R. Ambedkar[1] (1891-1956) discusses the issue of the relationship between nationalism and religion with a focus on Islam in India. He gives a very insightful account. Unfortunately, this book is not read as much as it should be.

Nationalism calls for loyalty to one's country. A country-based identity is glorified. The identity of being an Indian comes first for many Indians, and then come other identities such as religion, language and caste. But in Islam, a lot of importance is given to the sense of community of Muslims, which is called ummah. Loyalty to the community is more important than any other loyalty. Loyalty to Islam is more important than loyalty to a country. It is theoretically difficult for a Muslim to say, "I am an Indian first" whereas a Hindu can easily say, "I am an Indian first."

Ambedkar says, "Islam does not recognise territorial affinities. Its affinities are social and religious and, therefore, extraterritorial" (p. 42). We are not passing any moral judgements on the Muslims here, we are only examining their belief structure to look at the implications of it. To Muslims, their Muslim community is important and not any other identity.

The next thing is, that Muslims clearly distinguish themselves from the people of other religions. Islam favours Muslims highly over people of other religions. But Jews and Christians are given some respect, they are called the 'People of the Book' because Prophet Mohammed said that Jews and Christians have been given sacred books earlier, and they had prophets, and he was the last prophet in that line.

Jews and Christians are the People of the Book. They are not regarded as kafirs, meaning infidels or disbelievers. These infidels are a different category. To all Muslims, the Muslims first, next come the People of the Book, then you have others, worshippers of various gods, polytheists, idolaters, and pagans. Hindus come under this last category of pagans and idolaters. One can interpret Hinduism to mean that Hindus also worship one God, all kinds of interpretations are possible about Hinduism, but usually, the Hindus are considered polytheists and idolaters. Muslims theoretically need not give any respect to Hindus.

Many Muslims tend to think that Hindus are kafirs. Ambedkar says, "To the Muslims, a Hindu is a kafir. A kafir is not worthy of respect. He is a low-born and without status" (p. 330). The Quran says so many gruesome things about how kafirs should be treated, how they should be killed and burnt and so on.

Islam is not confined to spirituality. Islam as a religion aims to encompass the whole society. It is a very political religion. That's how Islam spread. Politics and religion are not distinguished in Islam. One of Prophet Mohammed's claims to prophethood is that he was successful in wars. He could win wars with fewer soldiers than the enemy. War, conquest, politics, and violence are all part of religion in Islam. Prophet Mohammed was much different from Jesus or Buddha who was only mostly preaching.

Muslims classify a country either as an abode of Islam or an abode of war. Dar-ul-Islam is an abode of Islam, and Dar-ul-Harb is an abode of war. If people are free to practise Islam in a country and the rulers are Muslims, then it is Dar-ul-Islam. If the rulers are infidels, then it becomes mandatory for the Muslims living in that country to try to change Dar-ul-Harb to Dar-ul-Islam.

Ambedkar says, "Hijrat (migration) is not the only way of escape to Muslims who find themselves in a Dar-ul-Harb. There is another injunction of Muslim Canon Law called Jihad (crusade). Jihad, migration – these are all ways by which Dar-ul-Harb could change to Dar-ul-Islam." Ambedkar says, "Technically, it is the duty of the Muslim ruler, who is capable of doing so, to transform Dar-ul-Harb into Daru-ul-Islam" (p. 323).

Situation in India

We had in India, before 1947, a large number of conservative Muslims who wondered whether India was Dar-ul-Islam or Dar-ul-Harb. They were likely to think that a Hindu rule will turn the country to Dar-ul-Harb. What kind of loyalty towards India could one have expected from these Muslims?

During the Khilafat agitation, the Muslims were mobilised for the first time in India, but not regarding the issues confronting them in India, it was regarding the issues confronting Muslims elsewhere. That is what is meant by the ummah, which gave rise to a pan-Islamic movement.

Ambedkar says, "The Indian Muslims who were carrying on the Khilafat movement actually went to the length of inviting the Amir of Afghanistan to invade India" (p. 114). "In this connection, attention must be drawn to the stand taken by the Muslim League. It is to the effect that the Indian Army shall not be used against Muslim powers" (p. 115).

Ambedkar says this attitude of Muslims is very dangerous for the country. A good Indian army cannot have people who are more loyal to Islam than to their country, who think that Hindus are kafirs, who think that a huge Islamic state needs to be created, and who long for the return of the glorious days of the Islamic empire that was there in India before the British rule.

Ambedkar gives a variety of reasons why India should be partitioned. Throughout the 530 pages of this book, he uses many arguments to appeal to Hindus about the need for partition: let them go, let them go, let them go. Ambedkar is clearly saying: please leave the Muslims because they are dangerous. Our army would be compromised if it had Muslims, who would be disloyal to the country. Their presence will weaken the army. He said that an unsafe army is more dangerous than unsafe borders.

Ambedkar says, "The realist must take note of the fact that Muslims look upon the Hindus as kafirs who deserve to be exterminated than protected." He goes on to say, "The realist must take note of the fact that while the Muslim accepts the European as his superior, he looks upon the Hindu as his inferior." About the presence of Muslims in the Indian army, Ambedkar notes, "It is doubtful how far a regiment of Muslims will accept the authority of their Hindu officers if they are placed under them" (p. 114).

And even if some Muslims are not disloyal to the nation, to begin with, they would still be susceptible to Islamic propaganda. Ambedkar says, "The realist must take note that of all the Muslims, the Muslims of the North-West is the most dissatisfied Muslim in his relation with the Hindus. The realist must note that the Punjabi Muslim is fully susceptible to the propaganda in favour of Pan-Islamism." Ambedkar repeatedly expresses his fear that any Muslim in the Indian Army could turn out to be treacherous. He says, "He would be a bold Hindu who would say that in any invasion by Muslim countries, the Muslims in the Indian army would be loyal and that there is no danger of their going over to the invader" (p. 114).

Ambedkar was not the only one who looked straight at the facts in this matter. He quotes Annie Besant who feared the subversiveness of Muslims at the time of the Khilafat movement. She said, "We have heard Muslim leaders declare that if Afghans invaded India, they would join their fellow believers, and would slay Hindus who defended their motherland... The claim now put forward by Muslim leaders that they must obey the laws of their particular prophet above the laws of the State in which they live, is subversive of civic order and stability of the State. It makes them bad citizens for their centre of allegiance is outside the nation."

Annie Besant was very clear about the threat Muslims would pose to a free India. She wrote, "If India were independent, the Muslim part of the population – for the ignorant masses would follow those who appealed to them in the name of their prophet – would become an immediate peril to India's freedom." She was very clear about where their allegiance lies. "Allying themselves with Afghanistan, Baluchistan, Persia, Iraq, Arabia and Egypt and with such of the tribes of Central Asia who are Muslims, they would rise to place India under the rule of Islam."

Some of the more educated sections of the Muslim populace might take the side of India, but they would be few and far between, and their resistance of fellow Muslims would be ineffective. "Some of the educated class might strive to prevent such a Muslim uprising. But they are too few for effective resistance and would be murdered as apostates" (p. 299).

Ambedkar, Annie Besant and some others knew why the presence of Muslims in this country was going to be a problem and how their disloyalty to the nation was going to be a serious issue after independence. Ambedkar quotes C R Das and he even quotes Rabindranath Tagore in this context.

Reporting an interview with Rabindranath Tagore, in 1924, a Bengali newspaper says, "A very important factor which, according to the poet, was making it almost impossible for the Hindu-Muslim unity to become an accomplished fact was that the Muslims could not confine their patriotism to any one country." It further says, "The poet said that he had very frankly asked many Muslims whether, in the event of any Muslim power invading India, they would stand side by side with their Hindu neighbours to defend their common land. He could not be satisfied with the reply he got from them. He said that he could definitely state that even such men as Mahomed Ali declared that under no circumstances was it permissible for any Muslim, whatever his country might be, to stand against any other Muslim." (p: 301)

Ambedkar thought that the partition was unavoidable, though it would not completely solve the communal problem. "Without Pakistan, the communal problem in India involves 6 ½ crores of Muslims, with the creation of Pakistan, it will involve only 2 crores of Muslims" (p. 134).

Think on it

1. Is Islam compatible with nationalism?
2. Is Islam compatible with equality and tolerance?
3. Is Islam compatible with democracy?
4. Wasn't partition of India a better idea if India wanted to be strong?
5. Do you agree with Ambedkar's views on the issue of Islam in India?

[1] Ambedkar's disagreement with Gandhi on caste-related issues and his conversion to Buddhism were covered in detail in my book Caste & Religion in India.

CHAPTER TWENTY

Pakistan Was Neither Sudden Nor Unnatural

Ambedkar said there was nothing sudden about Pakistan, he found the idea of Pakistan very natural and inevitable. Why did Ambedkar think so? He was taking into consideration the religious identities of people and the power of those identities. He was taking into consideration the historical hostilities between Hindus and Muslims and the unbridgeable gap between the two.

Historically, Muslim raids, the devastation they caused, and the consequent Muslim rule led to the antagonism between Hindus and Muslims. Ambedkar talks about the destruction of temples, forced conversions, and abasement of men and women. Ambedkar's historical references are: "Indian Islam" by Murry T Titus and "Medieval India Under Mohammaden Rule, 712--1764" by Stanley Lane-Poole.

Ambedkar writes in his book Pakistan or Partition of India, "The methods adopted by the invaders have left behind them their aftermath. One aftermath is the bitterness the Hindus and the Muslims which they have caused. This bitterness between the two is so deep-seated that a century of political life has neither succeeded in assuaging it, nor in making people forget it."

"As the invasions were accompanied with destruction of temples and forced conversions, with spoliation of property, with slaughter, enslavement and abasement of men, women and children, what wonder if the memory of these invasions has ever remained green, as a source of pride to the Muslims and as a source of shame to the Hindus?" (p. 80)

Next came British rule. Ambedkar says that the British rule altered the power balance between Hindus and Muslims in favour of the Hindus. Muslims had been the rulers during the medieval period, and now they became the subjects of the British just as the Hindus were. Many Muslims were upset that from being rulers of Hindus they became equals to them. They feared if India gets independence and if Hindus come to rule, then the Muslims will be subjected to Hindu rule.

Ambedkar writes, "The British conquest of India brought about a complete political revolution in the relative position of the two communities. For six hundred years, the Muslims had been the master of the Hindus. The British occupation brought them down to the level of the Hindus. From master to fellow subjects was degradation enough but a change from the status of fellow subjects to that of subjects of the Hindus is real humiliation" (p. 63).

Ambedkar says the idea of the ummah, which led to pan-Islamic movements, may provide great support to Muslims. The idea of Pakistan "opens up the possibilities of realising the Muslim idea of linking up all the Muslim kindred in one Islamic State and thus avert the danger of Muslims in different countries adopting the nationality of any country to which they belong and thereby bringing about the disintegration of the 'Islamic brotherhood'" (p. 364). Long before independence, some Muslims in India saw a kind of Islamic state was possible. A part of India could become a part of such an Islamic state.

Ambedkar also refers to social segregation between Hindus and Muslims. "It cannot but be a matter of the deepest regret to every Indian that there is no social tie to draw them together. There is no inter-dining and no intermarriage between the two. Their festivals are different. Their cultures are different; their literature and histories are different. They are not only different but, so distasteful to each other. No common meeting exists. None can be cultivated. There is not even sufficient physical contact. Wherever they live, they live apart. Every town and every village has its Hindu quarters and Muslim quarters, which are quite separate from each other. There is no common continuous cycle of participation."

Ambedkar continues, "They meet to trade or they meet to murder. They do not meet to befriend each another. When there is peace, the Hindu quarters and the Muslim quarters appear like two alien settlements. The moment war is declared, the settlements become armed camps" (p. 376).

Ambedkar also brings out the role of purdah or burkha in increasing this segregation. "Purdah is responsible for the social segregation of Hindus from Muslims. The Hindus are right when they say that it is not possible to establish social contact between Hindus and Muslims because such contact can only mean contact between women from one side and men from the other" (p. 252).

Then Ambedkar traces the history of the idea of Pakistan. "The idea underlying the scheme of Pakistan had taken birth sometime before 1923" "In 1930, leaflets and circulars were issued and set around to members of the R.T.C. in support of Pakistan" (p. 367).

It would be wrong to say that the idea just started in 1940 with the Pakistan resolution, without any background. Ambedkar didn't think that any concessions in power-sharing would have avoided partition. Indian historians consider Jinnah to be the most important person behind the creation of Pakistan. According to Ambedkar, Jinnah himself was shocked and swept off his feet by the power of the idea of Pakistan. He was not the originator of it.

"It is possible that the Muslims, in the beginning, thought that this destiny was just a dream incapable of realisation." (p 367) "It is far more possible that the Muslim leaders did not until very recently know the philosophical justification for Pakistan" (p. 368).

Ambedkar writes, "The Muslims appear to have started new worship of a new destiny for the first time. This is really not so. The worship is new because the sun of their new destiny which was so hidden in the clouds has only now made its appearance in full glow. The magnetism of this destiny cannot but draw the Muslims towards it. The pull is so great that even men like Mr Jinnah have been violently shaken and have not been able to resist its force" (p. 363).

Ambedkar writes, "In so segregating themselves, the Muslims were influenced by some mysterious feeling, the source of which they could not see but which was, all the same, directing them to keep apart from Hindus. This mysterious feeling and this hidden hand were no other than their pre-appointed destiny, symbolised by Pakistan., which unknown to them, was working within them. Thus viewed, there is nothing new or nothing sudden in the idea of Pakistan. The only thing that has happened is that, what was indistinct appears now in the full glow and what was nameless has taken a name" (p. 371).

Blaming the British for Pakistan does not make sense either. "The Hindus say that the British policy of divide and rule is the real cause of this failure. The Hindus having cultivated the Irish mentality to have no other politics except that of being always against the government, are ready to blame the government for everything including bad weather" (p. 361).

Think on it

1.   Was partition avoidable?
2.   Was partition desirable?
3.   Did Jinnah start the movement for Pakistan?
4.   Do you accept that burkha is an important element in the segregation of Hindu and Muslim communities?
5.   If partition had been accepted by the Congress early enough, could Pakistan have been created with lesser amount of violence?

Mohammed Ali Jinnah

CHAPTER TWENTY-ONE

Was Not Partition Unavoidable?

Mohammed Ali Jinnah (1876–1948) is a very controversial person in India. Both in India and Pakistan there is not much clarity on what he thought about, why he wanted Pakistan, what kind of Pakistan he envisaged, and to what extent he was responsible for the partition of India. These are highly contested issues.

At one time Jinnah wanted a secular, united and democratic India. He was called the ambassador of Hindu-Muslim unity by such people as Gokhale, Tilak, and Sarojini Naidu. On the other hand, Aga Khan, the president of the Muslim League wrote about Jinnah: "Who was our doughtiest opponent in 1906? A distinguished Muslim Barrister in Bombay, with a large and prosperous practice, Mr Mohammad Ali Jinnah. He said that our principle of separate electorate was dividing the nation against itself and for nearly a quarter of a century our most inflexible critic and opponent." Being critical of separate electorates, to which even Congress agreed at one time, means Jinnah believed that Hindus and Muslims could live in one state without any particular electoral safeguards for the Muslims.

Jinnah was at first opposed to joining the Muslim League. He was persuaded to become a member in 1913 after being assured that "his loyalty to the Muslim League and Muslim interest would in no way imply even the shadow of disloyalty to the larger national cause to which his life was dedicated." He was the main architect of the pact between Congress and the Muslim League in 1916.

Jinnah did not fear Hindu domination. During a Muslim League session in 1917, Jinnah said, "If 70 million Muslims do not approve of a measure, which is carried out by a ballot box, do you think it could be enforced and administered in this country? I say to my Muslim friends not to fear. This is a bogey put by your enemies to scare you away from the cooperation with the Hindus."

Gandhian phase

Jinnah imagined himself as the Muslim Gokhale. He was an important leader in Congress. He thought he would be a leader of a united, secular India. That seemed to be the destiny he wanted for himself. But his calculations were upset by none other than Gandhi. Jinnah could not get along with the Gandhian methods.

There were two things Jinnah didn't like about Gandhi. Jinnah advocated constitutional methods of reform, he felt that the Gandhian methods were very dangerous. He thought they didn't have any prospects. Jinnah grossly underestimated the power of Gandhism. The freedom struggle was entering a different phase, and Jinnah found himself out of tune with the times.

Jinnah also couldn't feel at ease with Gandhi's religious approach. He called it a "pseudo-religious approach to politics." Jinnah was against Gandhi taking up the Khilafat agitation. Jinnah turned out to be right on this point as it brought out the reactionary Muslim elements into mainstream politics. Gandhi was too naïve on this issue.

The Khilafat agitation was Gandhi's first movement. Only a few years ago did he come from South Africa to India. Gandhi didn't know that he was playing with fire. He thought that if the Muslims started taking part in the freedom struggle, they would continue to do so, and this would contribute to Hindu-Muslim unity. He was wrong and Jinnah was right.

It was during Gandhi's rise that Jinnah moved away from mainstream leadership, he ceased to be a leader of entire India. Till then Jinnah was not a leader of the Muslims, he was an important Congress leader who was also a Muslim, because of which he had some influence on the Muslim League and could mediate between the Congress party and the Muslim League. That was how he became "the ambassador of Hindu-Muslim unity".

As a leader of Muslims

In the new phase, Jinnah emerged as a representative of the Muslims in India. In 1928, we find a new Jinnah presenting his famous 14 points as an alternative to the Motilal Nehru Report, which advocated a joint electorate without sufficient safeguards for the Muslims. Jinnah's proposals included separate electorates and other safeguards such as representation in legislatures and cabinets both at the central level and the provincial level. But Congress found them unacceptable.

Jinnah now said about Hindu and Muslim differences, "If you do not settle this question today, we shall have to settle it tomorrow, but in the meantime, our national interests are bound to suffer." In the 2nd Round Table Conference (1931) he said, "I am an Indian first and a Muslim afterwards. But at the same time, I agree that no Indian can ever serve his country if he neglects the interests of the Muslims." One can see that at this point Jinnah's concern was the rights of Muslims in an undivided India.

Two-nation theory

As he went on speaking for safeguards for Muslims, Jinnah shifted to what was called the two-nation theory. The two-nation theory is often misunderstood. In the sense Jinnah used it, the word 'nation' referred to a distinct people, not to a state. Two-nation theory meant Hindus and Muslims are distinct as people. It did not automatically mean two states. Jinnah meant these were two peoples and without any safeguards for the minority, the Muslims would suffer. For these two distinct peoples to live under one state, the Muslims should have safeguards. That was his point.

Are Hindus and Muslims really two nations? Indeed they are, this is what Ambedkar too argued in Pakistan or Partition of India. Jinnah said: "The Hindus and Muslims belong to two different religious philosophies, social customs, literature. They neither intermarry nor dine together and, indeed, they belong to two different civilisations which are based mainly on conflicting ideas and conceptions. They derive their inspiration from different sources of history. They have different epics, different heroes and different episodes. Very often the hero of one is a foe of the other, their victories and defeats overlap." This is so true. Shivaji, for instance, is a hero to Hindus but a villain to Muslims. Ancient India reflects Hindus' glory, while medieval India brought out Muslims' glory.

In the Jan 1940 edition of Time and Tide, Jinnah wrote, "A plan of action must be evolved that recognises that there are in India two nations, but both must share the governance of their common motherland. In evolving such a constitution, the Muslims are ready to cooperate with the British government, the Congress so that the present enmities may cease and India may take its place among the great countries of the world."

To Jinnah, partition did not seem a logical solution to the issues raised by the two-nation theory. Muslims were spread across several states of India. Out of a total population of 6 1/2 crores, $1/3^{rd}$ were in the west, $1/3^{rd}$ were in the east and the remaining in what is present-day India. We can't assume that if somebody was asking for separate electoral rights for the Muslims, he would naturally seek partition. The western part could be separated, the eastern part too could be separated, but how about the rest? And there were a large number of Hindus in both these eastern and western areas. The issue was complicated. There were no easy solutions.

What Jinnah proposed was safeguards for the Muslims and a kind of devolution scheme where the centre would not have too much power. For the western part of India and the eastern part of India to be under closer control of the Muslims, the centre had to be less powerful because the centre would be controlled by the Hindus. Jinnah wanted such a political arrangement.

But why would Hindus agree to Jinnah's proposals – the safeguards and a weak centre? They constituted 80% of the population. If Hindus and Muslims constituted two nations, as they do, the partition of India was not avoidable. The Hindus wouldn't like to compromise on power and the Muslims would not want to live under Hindu domination.

If two states were created, the problem of majoritarianism would be minimised though not solved. It would still leave $1/3^{rd}$ of Muslims under Hindu domination. But in the end, partition turned out to be the only option, the last option, available to Jinnah.

It would be wrong to say Jinnah was responsible for the creation of Pakistan. He was simply responding to the situation he was in. As Ambedkar said, Jinnah was swept by the power of the idea of Pakistan, he was not the author of it. If Jinnah opposed the idea of partition, he wouldn't have remained a leader of Muslims. He became a great leader because he started advocating a cause that was dear to the Muslims.

On Pakistan

Scholars debate what kind of Pakistan Jinnah wanted. Pakistan turned out to be an Islamic country. I think here too what mattered was not what Jinnah wanted but what the attitudes of the people were. The hold of their religion is very strong on the Muslims. Leaders who raised the slogan of Islam became popular, because of which Pakistan turned Islamic.

In his Aug 11, 1947, speech made during the first session of Pakistan's constituent assembly, Jinnah said, "You may belong to any religion or caste or creed that has nothing to do with the fundamental principle that we are citizens and equal citizens of one state. In course of time, Hindus would cease to be Hindus, and Muslims would cease to be Muslims, not in the religious sense, because that is the personal faith of each individual, but in the political sense of the citizens of the state." This was a very clear statement in favour of a secular Pakistan. Jinnah appointed Jogendra Nath Mandal, an SC Hindu, as the first Law Minister. He commissioned Urdu poet Jagan Nath Azad, another Hindu, to write the national anthem.

If we consider Jinnah before the 1920s, his Western lifestyle and general belief system, it is reasonable to conclude that Jinnah wanted a secular Pakistan. Even after the formation of Pakistan, he remained essentially the same. That speech in the constituent assembly makes his secular vision clear.

But critics say Jinnah made speeches with conflicting ideas. In a Muslim League session in Delhi in 1943, for example, Jinnah said, "The constitution of Pakistan can only be framed by the millat and the people. The constitution and the government will be what the people will decide. The only question is that of minorities."

Even if Jinnah was interested only in the secular rights of the Muslims, and his only fear was Hindu domination, he did not make it clear that he wanted a secular Pakistan. He didn't use the word 'secular.' Probably such direct advocacy of secularism would have made him vulnerable to criticism by Islamists or dampened the enthusiasm among his followers. Whatever the reasons are, the state of Pakistan was created with an ideological ambiguity. Had Jinnah lived longer, surely it would have helped the cause of secularism in Pakistan, though we can't say Pakistan would not have become Islamic.

Think on it

1. How did Jinnah become an ambassador of Hindu-Muslim unity?
2. What was Jinnah's disagreement with Gandhi?
3. Since when did Jinnah start demanding electoral safeguards for Muslims?
4. What is meant by the two-nation theory?

5. To what extent was Jinnah responsible for partition?
6. Did Jinnah lead his people or was he led by them?
7. What factors contributed to the ideological ambiguity of Pakistan? And what were its consequences?

Jayaprakash Narayan

CHAPTER TWENTY-TWO

Gandhian Socialism

Jayaprakash Narayan (1902–79), also called Loknayak, evolved his ideas by combining Gandhism and socialism. At first, he was a Marxist, and when he was disillusioned with it he turned towards Gandhism. He played a part during the freedom struggle, and he lived long enough to see what was happening to that freedom.

Jayaprakash Narayan joined the national movement in 1921, as a teenager, quitting his studies. He wanted to dedicate his life to it, but when Gandhi called off the non-cooperation movement in 1922, JP left to study in the US. He didn't go there with much financial support, so he faced many financial troubles, because of which he had to move from one university to another, five in all, between 1922 to 29. This was also because of his changing interests, he started with science and finally moved to sociology. He completed his MA in sociology from the University of Wisconsin.

In the US he was influenced by Marxism. Also, he got a working experience that he would not have had had he stayed in India. He said, "In America, I worked in mines, factories and slaughterhouses. I worked as a shoeshine boy and even cleaned commodes in hotels. During vacations, I worked. Three or more boys lived in a single room and we cooked our food." He also read M N Roy on Marxism and colonialism.

JP came back to India when his mother was ill, in 1929. He was a Marxist and Marx did not believe in the concept of nations, but JP wanted to take part in the freedom struggle. He said, "The Indian communists said Gandhi is an agent of the capitalists. But they forgot Lenin." Lenin believed that the Marxists should cooperate with the leaders of the anti-colonial struggle.

Back in 1920, before JP left to the US, he married Prabhavati who was the daughter of a Gandhian. When JP was in the US, Prabhavati was in Gandhi's ashram. Prabhavati was a dedicated Gandhian. JP was jailed during the civil disobedience movement. Gandhi knew that JP did not believe in his methods, but Gandhi said about JP, "One day this man will speak my language."

JP played a very important role in the formation of the Congress Socialist Party in 1934. The Congress Socialist Party was a part of the Congress party and was expected to guide it toward socialism. JP wrote about his ideas on socialism in a book titled Why Socialism, published in 1936.

Over the years, JP changed his views on socialism as he got to know about the working of the USSR. He said, "Soviet revolution has two parts: the destruction of the old order of society and construction of the new. In a successful violent revolution, success lies in the destruction of the old order from the roots. That indeed is a great achievement." He continues, "... then there is need to create an organised means of violence to protect and defend the revolution. A new instrument of power is created and whosoever among the revolutionary succeeds in capturing this become new rulers. They become the masters of the new state and power passes from the hands of the people to them. There is always struggle for power at the top and the heads roll and blood flows."

"It is not that violent revolutionaries deceive and betray; it is just the logic of violence working itself out. It cannot be otherwise." He said, "Lenin attempted to realise socialism through violence and Stalin attempted to carry out a highly pressurised and forced process of industrialisation in a backward economy. This could not be accomplished without regimentation, compulsion and suppression of freedom."

In 1952-3, JP denounced the totalitarian distortions of socialism in Russia and blamed them "not only on heavy concentrations of political but also economic power." He said, "With the ghastly spectacle of the growth of totalitarianism with its leviathan state on a world scale we realised that decentralisation and devolution of economic power must be accepted as the essential tenet of democratic socialism."

JP delved into moral and ethical issues also. He believed man is a moral agent, man has spiritual needs. He wondered "if good ends could ever be achieved by bad means." From violence, you cannot get a nonviolent society.

JP took a stand against Marxist materialism. "Materialism as a philosophical outlook could not provide any basis for ethical conduct and any incentive for goodness." If the economy changes, all else will change, what should a man do? Marxism, "did not offer me an answer to the question: why should man be good?"

JP said, "Socialists should stop believing complacently when economic life had been socialised man would evolve automatically into a paragon of virtues." Socialised economic life means a socialist economy.

JP liked Gandhi's advocacy of village self-rule as well as Gandhi's critique of greed. From the 1950s, JP was increasingly drawn to Vinoba's work. JP was involved in Vinoba's Bhoodan movement in 1954 – which involved rich people voluntarily giving land to the poor. The state had no role in this.

JP said, "Socialism could not be created through law or force, but only through voluntary action." He even moved away from institutional politics, which he called 'raj niti' or power politics. He said we should move towards 'lok niti' or politics of the people. He rejected even party politics because a party is meant to capture and concentrate the power.

JP then retired from public life for many years. In 1974, he dramatically re-entered politics. He was arrested when an emergency was declared, in June 1975, and was released after a few months. Then JP, the man who opposed power politics, helped form a party that finally displaced Indira Gandhi. JP is largely remembered now for his role in politics during the emergency and also for his role during the Quit India movement three decades earlier, when he escaped from the jail and made many speeches asking the people to rebel against the British government.

Think on it

1. When did JP take part in the freedom struggle for the first time?
2. Why was JP disillusioned with Marxism?
3. According to JP, does man have spiritual needs?
4. Why was JP against Marxist materialism?
5. How is raj niti opposed to lok niti in JP's thought?

CHAPTER TWENTY-THREE

The Concept of Sarvodaya

JP's ideal world can be understood by his description of the Naga society. I found that JP's admiration of the Naga society makes his ideas much clearer than much of what he wrote on political and economic ideals.

On 30 January 1965, which was Gandhi's death anniversary, JP gave a speech in Patna on the Naga society. He became familiar with the Naga society because he was part of a three-member peace mission to Nagaland. The Nagas at one time were involved in a secessionist struggle and they resorted to violence. JP visited Nagaland to hold talks with them. He liked many things about the Naga society, he particularly liked village self-rule there.

JP said, "Gandhi used often to talk of village self-rule. If you want to see village self-rule in practice, go to Nagaland. The way those villages run their affairs, the strength they display, is truly admirable." He said, "The government of Nagaland wants the village council of Kohima to give it land. They say the government can't take over the land without the consent of the village council." JP asked, "But what is the situation in other states? The government can uproot village after village without taking anyone's permission."

In the Naga society, the village decides. It has control over its resources. It creates common properties. JP said, "Near the town of Mokokchung is a village named Ungma. About 4000 people are residents there. There is a very big church. It has a seating capacity of 5000. You will be astonished to learn that the church was built entirely by the voluntary labour of villagers. They used no material nor any expertise from outside." JP then says, "Not just this church, even high schools were built by the villagers themselves."

They had a healthy attitude towards labour. JP says, "A Naga even if he has a BA or MA degree does not consider physical labour to be beneath his dignity. The deficiencies that one finds in educated elsewhere in India are absent there. If a boy comes home on holiday, he would happily help his parents in the fields or in housework. What we Gandhians try to teach under the rubric of 'basic education' is already part of the teaching there. The greatest quality of the Nagas is the dignity of labour in daily life, which we can learn from."

JP extended the idea of decentralisation even to union-state relations. He wanted the Centre to have only minimal functions related to coordination. "If Bihar had its own currency, and Bengal its own too, imagine what confusion would arise. Issues such as defence and foreign affairs must be the responsibility of the Centre. However, all other subjects must be within the control of the states. The situation today is such that without assistance from the Centre the states are not able to function. For schools, the Centre has to give them money."

When states have substantial powers, there would not be secessionist demands too. JP promised the same thing to the Nagas, "I kept on telling the Nagas that there is no need for you to demand a separate nation since you can be fully free within India." JP says, "The giving up of certain rights to the Centre is not done to permit India to subjugate the provinces, rather, to safeguard the Union of India."

In his book A Plea for the Reconstruction of Indian Polity (1959), he suggested five levels of polity – village, block, district, state and centre. He suggested not only interlinking the three levels of Panchayati Raj Institution but also linking the PRIs with legislatures at the state and union levels. "The district councils of the state would come together to create the state assembly. The state assemblies would bring into being the Lok Sabha." In the present arrangement, members of state assemblies and Lok Sabha are directly elected by the people.

JP believed that centralisation of power was a big issue in post-independence India. In Feb 1957, on the eve of the second general elections, he said "The most important issue this time is that of the absoluteness of Congress power. The concentration of every form of power must be destroyed." A month before the declaration of emergency, he said, "The present all-pervading corruption has its roots in politics and power." The chief task of the people is "to prevent power from being corrupted in the future."

The aim of the Sarvodaya is "to diffuse political and economic power and decentralise the politico-economic structure." Economically, JP believed in the framework of cooperatives, that workers can be part owners of an industrial set-up.

Democracy doesn't have much meaning when power is concentrated. Voters are "manipulated by powerful, centrally controlled parties, with the aid of high finance and diabolically clever methods and super media."

Lok Niti

JP believed in voluntarism. He emphasised lok niti over raj niti, saying, "Law can't come into effect without public opinion to enforce it. Legislation without conversion first is a dead letter." India's land reforms are an example.

JP says, "It is not institutions, not laws, not political systems, not constitutions which create good people. For that, you require a widespread process of education understood in the widest sense of the word. Education does not mean academic education; but the improvement of human beings through service, love, examples, preaching, reasoning and argument."

At that time there was a serious problem from dacoits in Madhya Pradesh. For more than 20 years, the dacoits had been operating out of the ravines and jungles of Madhya Pradesh. Repeated attempts to flush them out with troops and aerial bombardment failed. Then JP intervened. Expressing his belief that "any heart can be changed if the right approach is made," Narayan entered parleys with them. He convinced them that "the only way you will earn peace of mind is by changing your lives and purifying yourselves." About 400 of them surrendered to him. They were assured of fair trials. Though charged with murder, they were given only some years of imprisonment rather than a death sentence. This was the approach of Gandhi and Vinoba Bhave too, they trusted people. When asked if the leader of the dacoit gangs could stand for the parliament after release from prison, JP quipped, "He would not be in a good company, because he would be a reformed dacoit."

Sarvodaya

The word 'sarvodaya' comes from Sanskrit, 'sarva' and 'udaya' meaning 'all' and 'morning' – a new dawn for everyone, progress for all. JP was inspired by Ruskin's Unto This Last, it was the same book that inspired Gandhi. Gandhi coined this term 'sarvodaya' and it meant taking into consideration the wellbeing of the last man. Vinoba Bhave wrote, "Sarvodaya does not mean good government or majority rule, it means freedom from government, it means decentralisation of power." Sarvodaya implied decentralisation and harnessing the positive nature of man. Marx and Gandhi both believed that the state should finally wither away, but Sarvodaya meant not waiting for the withering away of the state, it is based on the premise of not depending on the state in the first place.

JP left party politics at some point. However, at the fag end of his life, he got involved in party politics again. JP gave a call for a total revolution in 1975. Though others were interested only in overthrowing Indira Gandhi, JP said we shouldn't stop there, we have to work to create a new society. This concept of total revolution came from Vinoba Bhave, who put forward a slogan in the 1960s: "To mould a new man to change human life and create a new world." But was there any real effort made in the direction of total revolution? Very little, because JP was aged and sick and was to die soon. JP remained a radical thinker till his death.

Think on it

1. How should an ideal village be, according to JP?
2. What is the importance of teaching dignity of labour to children?
3. What are JP's views on union-state relations?
4. What is the 5-tier polity that JP suggested?
5. Give two examples of lok niti that JP was involved with.
6. What is meant by Sarvodaya? Where did the concept come from?

Ram Manohar Lohia

CHAPTER TWENTY-FOUR

Affirmative Action as Socialism

There are many commonalities between Ram Manohar Lohia (1910–67) and Jayaprakash Narayan (1902–79). Both were socialists as well as Gandhians. Lohia was 8 years younger than JP but died 12 years earlier than him. Lohia went abroad for studies in 1929 and returned in 1933, whereas JP went abroad for studies in 1922 and returned in 1929.

Lohia was studying in Berlin, Germany while the civil disobedience movement was going on, and he followed it from there. He got his doctorate in 1932, it was titled 'Salt and Satyagraha'. Lohia studied a lot of Marxism, and when he came back to India, he joined the Congress Socialist Party (CSP), founded in 1934 by JP and others.

Lohia took part in the Quit India movement. He was imprisoned in 1944 at Lahore Fort jail, along with JP. Lohia was frequently involved in broadcasting during the Quit India movement. He became a member of Praja Socialist Party in 1952, along with JP. Till 1952, you can say that their journey was similar, but from then on they took different routes.

JP left party politics whereas Lohia remained a member of a political party. Lohia became an MP for the first time in 1963. Though he did not turn out to be a successful politician, his ideas inspired politics in post-independence India.

Lohia was more scholarly in his approach to politics than JP. Lohia did a PhD, whereas JP did M.A. in sociology. Lohia was more studious. By the '30s, the world knew more about the problems with Marxism, so Lohia could be a more systematic critic of it.

Rejecting the materialism of Marx, Lohia said that ideas also play an important role along with economic factors in shaping a society. Rejecting the concept of the universal applicability of Marxism, Lohia said societies don't follow a unilinear growth from primitive communism to communism. The idea of unilinear growth is less relevant outside Europe.

Lohia felt Marx did not pay enough attention to the link between capitalism and imperialism. To Lohia, capitalism and imperialism are closely linked. In the 1800s, when Britain was growing using capitalism as an economic ideology, it was facilitated by imperialism. Capitalist enterprises in European countries extracted more labour as surplus from the colonial countries than from their own countries.

Lohia said that Marxian predictions did not turn out to be true. In Europe, living standards improved and middle classes were formed, contrary to what Marx predicted. The failure of the Marxian predictions had been studied by Bernstein by then. Lohia also felt that Marx did not have a theory of nationalism. Lohia was a systematic critic of Marxism in theory not just of its application in the USSR.

Panchayati Raj Institutions

Lohia proposed a four-pillar state in the context of India. He said, "The next great advance in the constitution-making will be when a country frames its constitution on the basis of the four-pillar state, the village, the district, the province and the centre, being four pillars of equal majesty and dignity." Province means state. The block level in JP's model is not present here. There is a distribution of legislative as well as executive functions, including planning and production.

Big things like railways go to the centre, and small textile units go to the districts. Lohia said, "I need not add that a substantial part of state revenues should stay with the village and district." He also said, "Agriculture, industry and other property, which is nationalised, should as far as possible, be owned and administered by village, city and district panchayats."

Lohia knew the main problem with Gandhi's self-sufficient village, which is the absence of trade. "The concept of self-sufficiency had better be eliminated. The village must stay in close relationship with numerous other villages and also the world at large."

Lohia defines democracy this way: "The greatest single quality of democracy in the present age of decentralisation and its meaning must be fixed both in terms of defined political power belonging to small units of direct democracy and economic arrangements and technology that would give the working man greater understanding of control over the productive process." The scale of technology was important to him, as it affected the level of decentralisation and the degree of democracy.

Lohia advocated giving the bottom level maximum power that can yet be consistent with the integrity of the nation. "As to the decentralisation of political power, the principle may be laid down straight away as one of the maximum divisible powers to the village or the city consistent with the integrity and unity of the country."

Lohia defines socialism this way: "If socialism is to be defined in two words then they are, equality and prosperity. I do not know if this definition has been given earlier at any time. If so, I would call it the best definition given so far." Lohia wanted equality not in poverty but in prosperity. Lohia believed it was possible.

To this ideal polity, Lohia also added certain moral aspects, like Satyagraha which meant settling conflict through nonviolence. He believed that the right means are needed for the right ends.

Lohia advocated land reforms. He also said that limits should be imposed on incomes as well as expenditures. He believed that there should not be too much inequality between the incomes of the rich and the poor. He proposed that there be just one class in railways. He suggested that for some years there should be a ban on cars for private use. The focus should be on public transport.

Role of state

While JP moved toward solving the issues without the help of the state, Lohia believed in the role of the state. If you say decentralise the government and let people rule themselves, you would be relying on society to rectify itself. Lohia says that decentralisation is needed but the society is not good enough to take care of itself. The state is needed to change society.

So Lohia believed in the state reforming the society. We can say Ambedkar would agree about this approach. When Gandhi proposed self-ruling villages, Ambedkar disagreed. The Gandhian approach is similar to that of JP, and Ambedkar's approach is similar to that of Lohia. Lohia and Ambedkar saw society as a problem and thought it cannot be left to itself.

Sapta Kranti

Lohia said that seven revolutions are needed to transform Indian society. The number seven is used here in a loose sense and meant many revolutions. Lohia said there is a great deal of discrimination based on gender, and this should be undone. This is one revolution. Similarly, there is discrimination based on ethnicity, caste and class, they should all be undone.

Normally socialists think that if class differences are taken care of, caste differences will be automatically taken care of. But while there might be a good deal of correspondence between some castes and classes, Lohia thought they should be treated separately. Ambedkar would agree.

Lohia said that affirmative action is needed to end these inequalities, it is one way of using the state to reform the society.

Caste-based reservation was a very important proposal that Lohia made. He also advocated ethnicity-based reservation and gender-based reservation. Reservations to women and SCs, STs and OBCs are important. Lohia thought that all SCs, STs and OBCs and women should be given reservations regardless of their religion. This reservation can go up to 60%.

Lohia was against language-based discrimination too. He was against the domination of the English-speaking elite. Lohia felt that Hindi should be promoted along with the regional languages. People should have the power to choose their own primary language of communication. "Power, including the right to choose its language of primary instruction and commerce should be given to the village community." However, Lohia wanted Hindi to be the link language and English to be progressively replaced.

Coming to Lohia's views on education, he believed in the dignity of labour. He said, "A large part of a child's initial instruction had to be woven around some form of agricultural or industrial activity." Every student should get a year's experience on a farm or a factory as a part of the undergraduate program.

Lohia was an atheist but was not against religion. He said, "Religion is long-term politics and politics is short-term religion." You can see from his acceptance of Gandhism that he believed religion could be a source of ethics. But unlike Gandhi, Lohia wanted to see criticism of religion. He said that the Indian mind should have "patience to hear criticisms of Rama or Muhammad." It should not "spill blood or burn books." Lohia wanted different versions of Ramayana and Mahabharata to be heard and discussed among the people. They are after all myths. Different classes can take different versions, not everybody has to believe in Valmiki's Ramayana. This is an unusual view.

The fight against inequalities should never be at the expense of civil liberties. In the context of freedom of women, he praised Sweden that had hospitals with placards, "Unmarried mothers are given special care." He didn't think of morality the way a conservative Hindu would.

Lohia wanted equality across nations as well. To his four-pillar state, he added another pillar at a fifth level: the world government. He wanted barrier-free movement of people across nations. He also wanted countries to have smaller armies. He wanted a world parliament to be formed based on adult franchise. He envisaged the eventual formation of a world government. Despite having such grand ideas, he never criticised what India was doing in the context of Jammu & Kashmir. His views on internationalism also do not go well with his opposition to English. If he wanted the citizens to have an international outlook, then English would help and not Hindi.

Think on it

1. What were the similarities between JP and Lohia?
2. What was Lohia's criticism of Marxism?
3. What is Lohia's four-pillar state?
4. What does the four-pillar state say about ownership of industry?
5. Why was Lohia against the idea of a self-sufficient village?
6. What were Lohia's views on technology?
7. Did Lohia believe in placing limits on expenditures of people? Is that a good idea?
8. What is Sapta Kranti?
9. How were Lohia's views on caste different from that of a Marxist?
10. What is the role of affirmative action in Lohia's socialism?
11. What were Lohia's views on religion?
12. What were Lohia's views on the role of the English language?
13. What were Lohia's views on internationalism?

Jawaharlal Nehru

CHAPTER TWENTY-FIVE

Socialism: Where Most Indian Thinkers Failed

Socialism was taken as a great ideal in India and was not debated much. Prime Minister Nehru was very much committed to the cause of socialism. Only when India faced a huge economic crisis in 1991 did we change our policies. Many people started rethinking the path of socialism that India had followed for decades. The USSR collapsed in 1991 because of its socialism, and earlier in 1979 China too took to market reforms thus moving away from socialism.

After independence, not many opposed the path of socialism that India was embarking on. Rajagopalachari was one of those few who seem to have understood the problem with socialism during Nehru's time. He started a new party advocating pro-market ideology.

Jawaharlal Nehru (1889–1964) was a very strong advocate of socialism in India. When he was studying at Cambridge and Harrow in England, he attended lectures by political and economic thinkers such as Bertrand Russell and JM Keynes. Nehru was not a dogmatic Marxist, he understood Marxism as well as alternative economic ideologies. However, he came to favour socialism in the context of India.

In his book The Discovery of India, Nehru wrote: "Economic change will have to be in the direction of a democratically planned collectivism." He clarifies: "A democratic-collectivism need not mean the abolition of private property, but it will mean the public ownership of the basic and major industries. In India especially it will be necessary to have, in addition to the big industries, cooperatively controlled small and village industries. Such a system of democratic collectivism will need careful and continuous planning and adaptation of the changing needs of the people."

The problem is that generally there would not be much incentive for an individual to do more in any collective ownership. Also, state-owned enterprises are managed by the political sector and if the political sector becomes corrupt and inefficient, then the public sector will also become corrupt and inefficient. In Nehru's socialism, there was not much scope for the private initiative which inhibited wealth generation.

Nehru did not think that the government had to play a role only for a limited period till the private sector developed. He thought all the important industries should be in the public sector. Nehru created a huge public sector. The public sector means an industry controlled by the government and managed by officers. It was centrally planned. Nehru was following the Soviet model but in the context of democracy.

Rajaji's criticism

C. Rajagopalachari (1878–1972), popularly known as Rajaji, understood that there was a serious problem with Nehru's approach. Rajaji was the first Indian Governor General, he was a freedom fighter and was quite close to Gandhi and Nehru. He was the chief minister of Madras till 1954. He formed the Swatantra Party in 1959. If you read what he said on this topic, then you will know that many inefficient things crept into Nehru's socialist model by the 1960s.

Rajaji said in 1959, "Private enterprise should be fostered by every means available and not treated as a dangerous enemy. Industrial enterprise would then spread at various levels in the countryside and reduce the tensions that attach to centralised industrialism." Private sector participation would lead to decentralised production which would promote democracy.

Rajaji said, "The role of the government should be that of a catalyst in stimulating economic development while individual initiative and enterprise are given the fullest play." He said, "Economic development takes place faster when diversity is permitted and fullest use of is made of local, physical and social conditions by those who know them." The market would respond to local conditions.

C. Rajagopalachari

Centralisation gave rise to complex procedures. Rajaji said, "One of the most neglected aspects of planning in this country is the gearing up of the administrative machinery and the simplification of procedures." What Rajaji wrote in 1959 was realised to some extent only in the 1990s, after economic liberalisation. It would seem like Rajaji was at least 30 years ahead of his time in his views on the economy.

At the time of launching the Swatantra Party in 1959, Rajaji issued its manifesto. It said, "The Swatantra Party stands for minimum government and minimum state interference, for minimum expenditure in administration and for minimum taxation, for minimum interference in the private and professional affairs of citizens and for minimum regulation in industry and trade." This minimum intervention would pave the way for the economic freedom of individuals.

Rajaji said, "Responsibility is reduced if the individual disappears and multiple ownership and delegated authority take over the management." Public management reduces the responsibility of individuals and makes the economy inefficient. Rajaji said, "Egalitarian distribution of distress and poverty is not what anybody wants." Egalitarian distribution of wealth is what is needed and not poverty.

State control simply means control by the ruling party, which can use the public sector for its ends. "It is not good for the nation to allow the states which be it remembered must always be in the grip of some political party with its own motives and interests, to run all the beneficent activities of the nation as its exclusive monopoly."

Rajaji's manifesto says, "The Swatantra Party believes that social justice and welfare can be reached more certainly and properly in other ways than through the techniques of so-called socialism with all its accomplishments of injustice, expropriation and repudiation of obligations." Why was socialism a repudiation of obligations? In the kind of socialism that was implemented in India, one did not face punishment when one did not do one's duty.

The manifesto said: "The party would restrict state enterprise to heavy industries to supplement private enterprise in that field, national services such as the railways, and the starting of pioneer industries where private initiative is lacking." The private initiative will be encouraged as much as possible, and the public sector will be involved only where private enterprise cannot take the lead.

The manifesto said: "The party wants taxation to be kept at a level which is not so high that exacting as to prevent the capital formation and investment by individuals." This was indeed done but during the 1990s.

By the early 60s, the License Raj prevailing in India made honest enterprising people live in fear, and Rajaji writes in an essay titled India I Want (1961), "I want an India clear of the atmosphere of fear in which it is now enveloped, where honest men engaged in the difficult tasks of production or trade can carry on their occupation without fear of ruin at the hands of officials, ministers and party bosses."

"I want an India where talent and energy can find scope for play without having to cringe and obtain special individual permission from officials and ministers, and where their efforts will be judged by the open market in India and abroad." "I want the corruption of this permit-licence raj to go."

Rajaji says, "I want real equal opportunities for all and no private monopolies created by the permit-license raj." Nehru assumed that the free market would create monopolies, but Rajaji was saying that it was the state that was creating the monopolies, by favouring some people over others.

The idea that under socialism the state would be free from business pressures is not true, as big businesses can bribe the government to get licenses. Rajaji says, "I want the money power of big business to be isolated from politics."

Nehru couldn't avoid what he thought he would avoid through socialism – the monopolies, the corruption, and big money playing part in politics. Rajaji was saying that it was Nehru's socialism that brought all of these evils. If that was the case by the 60s, later the political sector deteriorated further and the problems of socialism worsened.

If the socialism of Nehru was wrong, was the one advocated by JP and Lohia right? Both JP and Lohia were against only centralization and not against public ownership. They too would be equally wrong. Lohia's proposals on placing limits on both incomes and expenditures of all classes of people would have made things far worse if implemented. Nehru, Lohia and JP never understood the power of the free market. Lohia's advocacy of affirmative action as a part of socialism is a different issue. Gandhi and Nehru had many arguments on the desirable direction of the economy. Gandhi criticized industrialism and not public ownership.

Think on it

1. What was socialism to Nehru? Why did he adopt the socialist model for India?
2. What could be the central problem in any collective production system?
3. What are the problems with centralised planning?
4. What are the advantages of a free market?
5. How could socialism end up creating monopolies?
6. How could socialism make money play a big role in politics?
7. Was the socialism of JP and Lohia better than that of Nehru?
8. Did Gandhi criticise collective ownership of industries?

Hindutva

V.D. Savarkar

CHAPTER TWENTY-SIX

Savarkar's Concept of Hindutva

Let us discuss the concept of Hindutva as propounded by V.D. Savarkar (1883-1966). Some people use the word 'Hindutva' simply to refer to anything related to Hinduism. They use it in an inclusive sense, but Savarkar's use of the word 'Hindutva' has specific connotations[1].

Savarkar's concept of Hindutva can be discussed in terms of some particular assumptions and proposals. Firstly, he takes the position that Hindus and Muslims can never be part of one nation. They have been historically antagonistic to each other. He said, "Hindus and Muslims are two antagonistic nations living side by side." They were so in the past, they are so now and they will remain so in the future. To think that they were not so is wrong, to think that they can be welded into one nation is wrong. Savarkar said, "Several infantile politicians commit the serious mistake in supposing that India is already welded into a harmonious nation or that it could be welded thus for the mere wish of doing so."

That Hindus and Muslims have been antagonistic to each other was an observation made by both Jinnah and by Ambedkar, but Savarkar's position was different. Savarkar introduces a certain new concept. He defines India as the geographical region stretching from the Indus river to the seas, and the Hindus in India take this land as their punya bhumi, the holy land, and pitru bhoomi, their fatherland. Only the Hindus of this country take India as their holy land and fatherland.

The concept of 'holy land' refers to a place where the religion of a people is coming from. The Hindu religion is coming from this land only, so to the Hindus, this is their holy land. And the term 'fatherland' refers to a place where the culture of a people is coming from, including the language and social norms. To the Hindus, India is their fatherland. But to the Muslims of India, this country could only be their fatherland at the most, and not the holy land. Their holy land is the geographical region comprising Mecca and Madina. Using this terminology, to the Buddhists in Japan and China, India would be their holy land, but not the fatherland.

Savarkar says, because India is the holy land as well as the fatherland only to the Hindus, they are most loyal to the land, they have no extra-territorial loyalty. Muslims can't be as loyal to India.

Savarkar first says that Hindus take India as their holy land and fatherland. Then he says that Hindus should take it that way. The project of the Hindu Mahasabha is to promote the ideology of Hindutva which would make the Hindus proud of India. Savarkar said, "The Hindu Mahasabha is for the advancement and glory of Hindu Rashtra."

It is not only that the Muslims may not be as loyal as the Hindus, they can even work to wreck this nation. Savarkar thinks that Muslims can ally with other Muslims outside India to wreck this country. He said, "Thousands of Muslims could be found conspiring with Turkish Khailaphatists and Afghans with an object to bring a foreign invasion if but a Muslim rule could thus be established in this land."

Savarkar advocates that Hindus should vote for those leaders who are promoting the cause of Hinduism, and not for those who are saying religion doesn't matter to them or that Hindus and Muslims are equal. He said, "Hindus commit the suicidal blunder of voting for those who openly declare that they are neither Hindus nor Muslims. They must vote for those who are not ashamed of being Hindus, openly stand for the Hindus." The Hindus should not vote for the people who are championing secularism. "Muslims only vote for those who openly and boldly pledge to guard and aggressively secure rights for the Muslims."

The concept of Savarkar's Hindutva has these implications.

Think on it

1. What is a holy land?
2. What is a fatherland?
3. Why are the Hindus most loyal to India?
4. Why should Hindus be wary of Muslims?
5. What is the purpose of the Hindu Mahasabha?
6. Is Hinduism the same as Hindutva?

[1] All the quotations here are taken from Savarkar's presidential address to the Hindu Mahasabha in 1937, given in The Penguin Book of Modern Indian Speeches.

CHAPTER TWENTY-SEVEN

Golwalkar Calls for Ghar Wapsi

M.S. Golwalkar

M.S. Golwalkar (1906-73) is a very important thinker in the Hindutva school. He had been the chief of RSS for many years, from 1940 till his death in 1973. His philosophy is not different from that of Savarkar[1].

Firstly, Golwalkar believes a single culture is a source of strength to any nation. He said, "The people should have evolved a definite way of life moulded by the community of life-ideals, of culture, or feelings, sentiments, faith and traditions." Secondly, he believes that the people should have a love for their land. "They should have developed love and adoration for it as their motherland. They should feel that they are the children of the soil."

Savarkar takes the position that in India only Hindus have such love for their land. Golwalkar agrees. "It is the forefathers of the Hindu people who have set up standards and traditions of love and devotion for the motherland. It is they who shed their blood in defence of the sanctity and integrity of the motherland. It means that only the Hindu has been living here as the child of the soil."

This implies that to create a strong nation, the people of other cultures should change into Hindu culture. Golwalkar says that the Muslims should accept the Hindu culture to make India great. "Muslims should come back and identify themselves with the Hindu way of life in dress, customs, building homes, performing marriage ceremonies and funeral rites and such other things." His position is that after all they were Hindus once and they should come back to Hinduism. The Hindus should welcome them. This concept of return is called ghar wapsi or homecoming.

Golwalkar says the Muslims in India were dangerous before the creation of Pakistan, and they remain dangerous afterwards too. "It would be suicidal to delude ourselves into believing that Muslims have turned patriots overnight after the creation of Pakistan. On the contrary, the Muslim menace has increased a hundredfold by the creation of Pakistan which has become a springboard for all their future aggressive designs on our country."

This leads to a position that all Muslims in India, so long as they remain Muslims, are dangerous to India or they weaken India.

Think on it

1. What is Ghar Wapsi?
2. Why should Muslims change their ways?

3. Why is cultural homogeneity needed for a strong nation?

[1] The quotations are taken from Ramachndra Guha's selections from a compilation of Golwalkar's speeches, Bunch of Thoughts as given in Guha's Makers of Modern India.

CHAPTER TWENTY-EIGHT

Godse: Why I Killed Gandhi

Nathuram Godse

Nathuram Godse (1910–49) himself explained why he killed Gandhi, in his trial speech[1]. The core belief of Godse was that he didn't consider India belonged to both Hindus and Muslims. He believed this was Hindus' land and the Muslims took a part of it. The Muslims don't have any rights over this land. Godse felt a part of his motherland was being given to others.

Godse said, "Born in a devout Brahman family, I instinctively came to revere Hindu religion, Hindu history and Hindu culture. I began to devote myself to the study of Hindu Sanghanist ideology and program, which alone, I came to believe, could win and preserve the national independence of Hindustan, my motherland. When the top leaders of Congress, with the consent of Gandhi, divided and tore the country, which we consider a deity of worship, my mind was filled with direful anger."

Why was Gandhi targeted? For two reasons. First, Gandhi had been the leader of the freedom struggle, and so he was responsible for the consequences, including the partition. Godse said, "If the country wanted Gandhi's leadership, it had to accept his infallibility; if it didn't, he would stand aloof from the Congress and carry on his own way. Either Congress had to surrender its will to his and had to contend with playing the fiddle to all his eccentricity, whimsicality, metaphysics and primitive vision, or it had to carry on without him."

"Gandhi is being referred to as the Father of the Nation. But he acted very treacherously to the nation by his consenting to the partitioning of it. He has proved to be the Father of Pakistan."

Second, Gandhi's ideology of nonviolence was responsible for weakening the Hindus. "The Congress which had boasted of its nationalism and socialism secretly accepted Pakistan literally at the point of a bayonet and abjectly surrendered to Jinnah. Gandhi's inner voice, his spiritual power and his doctrine of non-violence of which so much is made, all crumbled before Jinnah's iron will and proved to powerless."

Savarkar also was critical of Gandhi's nonviolence. He said, in his address to Hindu Mahasabha in 1940, "Relative non-violence is doubtless a virtue. But absolute nonviolence, nonviolence under all circumstances and even when instead of helping human life whether individual or national it causes incalculable harm to humanity as a whole, ought to be condemned as a moral perversity."

But why kill Gandhi after the partition already happened? Godse disapproved of Gandhi's pro-Muslim attitude even after independence. Gandhi was always taking up the Muslim cause rather than the Hindu cause. Without Gandhi, Godse thought that India would be able to deal with Pakistan in a better way.

Godse said, "One of the conditions imposed by Gandhi for his breaking of the fast unto death related to the mosques in Delhi occupied by the Hindu refugees. But when Hindus in Pakistan were subjected to violent attacks he did not so much as utter a single word to protest." He said, "I felt the Indian politics in the absence of Gandhi would surely be proved practical, able to retaliate, and would be powerful with armed forces."

A better human than Savarkar

Savarkar was also put on trial for Gandhi's murder, but he was let off for want of corroborating evidence. Jeevanlal Kapur Commission,[2] constituted in 1969, three years after Savarkar's death, obtained evidence of the role Savarkar played in the plot to kill Gandhi. Whereas Godse was prepared to face death, Savarkar cleverly escaped the punishment he deserved for plotting to kill Gandhi. Collins and Lapierre, authors of Freedom at Midnight, described Savarkar in their book as "the zealot whose unseen hand had controlled the flow of at least three political assassinations" – those of Curzon Wilie, Jackson and Gandhi. Savarkar was convicted only in the Jackson case.

Savarkar would encourage others to murder but he would escape the consequences. When he was in Andaman jail, he wrote a series of mercy petitions to the British government because of which he had his prison sentence reduced.

He was jailed in 1911, and in the first year itself, he wrote a mercy petition, saying, "If the government in their manifold beneficence and mercy release me, I for one cannot but be the staunchest advocate of loyalty to the English government...

Moreover, my conversion to the constitutional line would bring back all those misled young men in India and abroad who were once looking up to me as their guide... I am ready to serve the government in any capacity they like, as my conversion is conscientious. The Mighty alone can afford to be merciful and therefore where else the prodigal son return but to the paternal doors of the government?"

Another one in 1920 said, "If the government wants further security from me then I and my brother are perfectly willing to give a pledge of not participating in politics for a definite period and reasonable period that the government would indicate." Savarkar was finally discharged and sent to Ratnagiri prison in Maharashtra in 1924. He was released later with some restrictions that remained till 1937.

How did Savarkar become Veer Savarkar? A biography of Savarkar came out in 1926 titled 'The Life of Barrister Savarkar' written by somebody called Chitragupta. It said, "Savarkar is a born hero, he could almost despise those who shirked duty for fear of consequences. If once he rightly or wrongly believed that a certain system of government was iniquitous, he felt no scruples in devising means to eradicate this evil. Savarkar seemed to possess no few distinctive marks of character, such as the amazing presence of mind, indomitable courage, and unconquerable confidence in his capability to achieve great things. Who could not help admiring his courage and presence of mind?"

In 1987 when this book was being republished with a preface by one Ravindra Ramdas, he made a startling revelation that Chitragupta was none other than Savarkar himself. So you write a book about yourself with an unidentified pseudonym and you praise yourself so much. The title of Veer was first used for Savarkar in this book.

Godse seems much more of an honest and simple person in comparison to Savarkar. Verrier Elwin, an anthropologist and a friend of Gandhi, who was present during Godse's trial noted in his diary that Godse's speech was the finest by a condemned man since Socrates's trial speech. G.D. Khosla, one of the judges in the trial said, "Had the audience of that day constituted into a jury they would have brought a verdict of 'not guilty ' by an overwhelming majority."

After encouraging Godse to murder Gandhi and face death, Savarkar decided to cut him off. Godse was hurt by Savarkar's attitude during the trial. P.L. Inamdar who defended the Godse brothers wrote in The Story of Red Fort Trial, 1948-49, "Nathuram was deeply hurt by Tatyarao's [Savarkar's] calculated, demonstrative non-association with him either in court or in Red Fort Jail. While the other accused freely talked to each other, Savarkar sat there in sphinx-like silence. Nathuram referred to his hurt feelings in this regard even during my last meeting with him at Simla High Court."

Those people of Hindutva keen on taking India away from Gandhi and towards Savarkar should ponder the meaning and implications of their agenda; it is not simply an ideological shift.

Think on it

1. Why did Godse think the partition was unfair?
2. What were Godse's complaints against Gandhi?
3. What was the need for Godse to kill Gandhi?
4. What was Savarkar's role in Gandhi's assassination?
5. Was Savarkar an honest man?

[1] The quotations are from Godse's 1949 trial speech 'Why I Killed Gandhi.'

[2] Based on A.G. Noorani's Savarkar and Hindutva and Pavan Kulkarni's articles in The Wire.

Dharmashastra

Dharma in Ancient Indian Political Thought

Dharma is a very important concept in ancient Indian political thought. Let's examine what's meant by dharma. Let's begin by considering how we pass a law. The parliament passes a law and the law deals with do's and don'ts. If you do what you are not expected to do, it will be considered an infringement and will lead to some punishment. The parliament deliberates on what's right and what's wrong and passes a law. But when we think that a certain law is not proper, then we will drop it or amend it. Law is based on what we think is right and wrong.

We also have something like a physical law. For example, there's Newton's second law, F = ma. It's not a law we made, it simply exists. We didn't choose it to be that way. Nor can we amend it or cancel it. We only discovered it. Based on this physical law, we can do many things, like we can build something.

Dharma is conceived as something similar to F = ma, something that already exists, something that is given, given by God or given by nature. It is not chosen by us. Dharma arises from the cosmic order. What happens when we don't consider F = ma? We would face certain losses. Who sees to it that we face these losses? That is a divine source, or that's just the nature of the physical universe. In the same way, if dharma is violated it will lead to disorder and losses.

In Sanskrit, the root word of dharma is dhri. It means to hold, to maintain, to preserve. Order is preserved through dharma. The following dharma is the way to maintain order in the human world. What does dharma consist of? Duties, responsibilities, and rights. This dharma is very closely linked to the religion of Hinduism. How does dharma impact a person? It impacts through consequences that a person faces during this life or in a life after this. If you do bad things, you would be punished during this life, but even if you are not, you would be punished in another life. Who ensures it is done? It is God, or simply the cosmic order. Thus dharma in Hindu political thought also calls for belief in karma, rebirth, heaven and hell. Sometimes dharma is also called law. It was also called rta in the Vedas.

The Hindus believe that there are four ends of life, the purushartha: dharma, artha, kama, and moksha. One should pursue artha or money, one can pursue kama or sensory pleasures, and in the end, one should pursue moksha. One should follow dharma always. Dharma applies to everybody, in the context of a family, a business, or an army; it is relevant for a brother, a father, a sister, or a king. Nobody is exempt.

This dharma is conveyed through Vedas, Upanishads, Puranas, Smritis, epics like Ramayana and Mahabharata, and Manusmriti. And there is also the Bhagavad Gita. These are dharma shastras. They convey a moral code. Think of what the Ramayana conveys on what a king should do, what a brother should do, and what a wife should do. In the Mahabharata, what kind of things did a person like Yudhisthira do, what kind of a role did Bheeshma play, why did Karna do what he did and what were the consequences? There is an undercurrent of what is dharma and the consequences of not following it in these epics.

Speaking of the dharma of a king, the king is supposed to protect the weak, see to the welfare of the people, and ensure the security of the people and their property. Ramayana shows how public opinion is important to a king. If the job is done well by a king, he will be blessed by the cosmic order.

Caste & Class

Now we have to question: Is dharma like F = ma? It does not seem so. We consider many things that were earlier regarded as dharma then as adharma now. A Brahmin was given a very high status compared to others. The worst status was that of the untouchables. The untouchables were meant to remain ignorant, only the Brahmins had the right to learn. We find such social arrangement to be adharma now. Same thing about gender issues, what was regarded as dharma for a wife in ancient times may not be regarded as dharma in modern times. But F = ma was just as true in ancient times as it is now.

Dharma is not really what it was thought to be, it did not originate in a divine source. A huge part of dharma is man-made. Some privileged people fabricated dharma in such a way that it was useful to them. Dharma is hugely favourable to the Brahmins. One very important aspect of dharma that was insisted upon by a king is maintaining the varna system. Each person was supposed to do only his duty and not any other kind of work even if it was more remunerative. Maintaining that caste order was a very important task of the king. That caste order gave the highest priority to the Brahmins.

Dharma was also more favourable to men as compared to women. It was based on the power structure. The Brahmins gave the idea that God himself was overseeing this code, to promote themselves. It turns out that all that was not divine law or cosmic order, it was simply an order that was created for the benefit of some people. Some of it contributed to the maintenance of social order and justice, but much of it was meant to uphold what we now regard as unjust.

Think on it

1. What is meant by dharma?
2. Who ensures punishment if dharma is violated?
3. What is the relationship of dharma with rebirth?
4. What are dharmasastras?
5. Was dharma influenced by the power structure? Explain.

Kautilya

CHAPTER THIRTY

Seven Elements of a State

Kautilya was a famous political thinker of ancient India. He served as the chief minister to Chandragupta who was the founder of the Mauryan dynasty. Chandragupta Maurya was the grandfather of Emperor Ashoka. It was Kautilya, also called Chanakya, who was responsible for the education of Chandragupta, and it was he who brought Chandragupta to power and established the Mauryan dynasty.

Chandragupta first had successes against some of the satraps of Alexander the Great who were ruling the west of the Indus. After winning the areas there, Chandragupta turned against the Nanda Empire and destroyed it. The Nanda Empire was on the east of the Indus. Chandragupta ruled over a large part of the Ganges, the Indus valley and a part of Deccan.

After his retirement, Kautilya wrote a very important political treatise called Arthasastra. This is dated around 300 BCE and was translated from Sanskrit only in the first decade of the twentieth century, by R Shyamasastry. The English version consists of two hundred thousand words, which makes a huge volume.

Arthasastra refers to the science of polity and wealth. The much broader dharmasastra also used to discuss them, but arthasastra is supposed to be a specialisation on polity and wealth.

Kautilya's Arthasastra deals with the realities of monarchy in a general form. There is no reference to any particular events. For most of the time, people lived in stateless societies. By Kautilya's time, states were formed. Kautilya discusses in Arthasastra the definition of state and its various elements. State is called rajya. Kautilya defines a kingdom or a state this way: "No territory deserves the name of kingdom unless it is full of people and controlled by an agglomeration of power with absolute authority over the territory."

Kautilya lists what he calls the angas or the limbs of the state. They are: swami, amatyas, janapada, durga, kosha, danda, and mitra or satru – totally 7 elements. This is called the Saptanga theory of the state. These elements are stated in the order of decreasing importance, the swami or the ruler is the most important element of the state, the amatyas or the ministers second important, and so on.

A particularly interesting aspect of Kautilya's view of the state is the inclusion of the neighbours, who may be friends or enemies, also as an element of the state. What lies outside the border is also an important aspect of the state that the king should take care of. In the various chapters or books of Arthasastra, Kautilya focuses on each of these elements of the state.

Seven elements

1. The first element is the king. The king is the face of the state. He should be very knowledgeable. He should have studied philosophy, the Vedic lore, economy, and polity. He should be familiar with the basics of various trades and professions. He should have the ability to learn from the people.

   The king should also have the right kind of mind, he should have control over the senses, he should shun vices like lust, anger and pride. He should be truthful, he should be righteous and disciplined as well as energetic. The king is supposed to have all these very good qualities. Kautilya says he should come from a noble family.

Kautilya is always particular about the varna dharma and family origins. If the king is from a noble family, he is more likely to be respected by the people at various levels of the social order.

Kautilya says that the happiness of the king lies in the happiness of the people. He is the preserver of dharma. Kautilya's ideal is a great king, a righteous king, one who thinks of the wellbeing of the people and one who intends to preserve dharma. But what an aspiring king may need to do to come to power and once in power to retain that power and outsmart his enemies is a different matter. Kautilya thinks that a king or an aspiring king should be in a position to use many strategies to retain or gain power.

1. Amatyas refers to the ministers who advise the king, but in a broader sense, it refers to all higher officials. It includes counsellors or executive heads. Kautilya says it is better if all these officials come from noble families and are native. Being native will help a minister to understand the people better and he would be more acceptable to others. The ministers are expected to be wise and gentle and possess good communication skills. They should be properly tested before being appointed. They should also be tested while in the office to check whether they can be corrupted.

2. The third element is janapada, which refers to territory and population. The territory is full of villages, with each village typically consisting of 100 to 500 houses and populated mostly by Shudra peasants. The revenue from the peasants is a huge source of income for the state. The king should encourage the people from other kingdoms to come and settle in the existing villages or new villages. There have to be mines to exploit the mineral wealth of the land, and timber should be extracted from the forests. The king should construct roads and maintain waterways and ports. He has to make the economy as productive as possible. A productive economy increases the tax income and which contributes to the power of the state.

4. The fourth element of the state is durga, which means fortified capital. At that time the capital cities were fortified to maintain security. A fortified city could additionally be surrounded by water on all sides, or by a desert or a thick forest. Or it could even be located on a mountain so that it remains inaccessible to the enemy.

5. Kosha means treasury. Money is needed to maintain the bureaucracy, to maintain the fort, and it is also needed to be able to stand the strain of expenditure during times of war and famines. There should be enough of surplus in the kosha.

Agriculture was very important source of revenue at that time. Farmers used to pay $1/6^{th}$ of their produce as tax. There were also the manufacturing and trade sectors, and so there were excise duties, customs duties and port charges. Kautilya says that farmers and traders should feel they are getting a fair deal. Taxation should not be heavy. Kautilya says the king should collect the taxes "just as the bees collect honey from flowers without damaging them in any way," or just as "the way calf drinks milk."

To meet unforeseen situations like a military expedition, a special levy can be imposed. Rich men can do more in terms of donations, and the king can give titles or honours in return. Even actors, singers, and prostitutes can pay up to half of their income to the state in an emergency.

6. Danda refers to army. Soldiers should be very good at war. They should be very loyal to the king. The majority of them should be from Kshatriyas. People from lower castes can join if they are brave. All the soldiers should have the power of endurance. They should be capable of undertaking long expeditions. They should be well trained in wielding a variety of weapons. Soldiers selected for permanent placement constitute the standing army. Kautilya says that the families of these soldiers should be kept happy.

Besides the standing army, sometimes hired or mercenary troops are raised. Troops from a friendly state could be taken, deserters from an enemy can be formed into an army unit. Some soldiers can be recruited from wild tribes. These different types of the army can be used for different purposes. Of all the types of the army, the standing army is the one on which the king depends the most. Each of the divisions and subdivisions in the army has its own flag, trumpets and drums so that each unit will develop its own identity and do its job well.

7. The seventh element is mitra. A dependable friend outside the state is important. This friendly king can be a near relative, a sahaja mitra, or he could be a cultivated friend, a kritrima mitra. He could be a neighbour or be adjacent to a neighbouring king. If a neighbouring king is your enemy, his enemy will be your friend. Whether a neighbouring state is a friend or an enemy and how powerful it is impact the foreign policy.

A good friend is powerful, consistent, and has common interests, He should be able to mobilise his forces to defend you in case of need. He shouldn't be the kind who could forsake you or even betray you. A good friend is a righteous man, he wouldn't cheat you. Kautilya wants the king to choose his friends with a lot of care and attention.

An effective state is a state in which all these seven elements are functioning harmoniously.

Think on it

1. How was Kautilya associated to the Mauryan dynasty?
2. How is arthasastra different from dharmasastra?
3. What is Kautilya's definition of state?
4. What are the seven elements of a state?
5. Who is an ideal king?

6. What is the role of amatyas?
7. What does Kautilya say on taxation?

CHAPTER THIRTY-ONE

Realist Foreign Policy

In Kautilya's Arthasastra, the 'vijigishu' plays an important role. Vijigishu refers to an ambitious king, who can also be considered a conqueror or an invader. He is a king who not only wants to retain his kingdom but also to expand it. In real life, to Kautilya that vijigishu was Chandragupta, whom he guided.

Of the 15 books in Arthasastra, what the vijigishu should do to expand his kingdom are given in book IX, book X and XIII. Book IX deals with the timing of the attack of a kingdom and the location of the attack. Kautilya gives a lot of importance to intelligence-gathering and exploiting the divisions within the enemy country. He gives importance to finding out who might be traitors to the king, and to how to employ spies. In Kautilya's scheme, an espionage network has an important role. Spies can be employed in the guise of doctors, mendicants, pilgrims, sadhus, and beautiful women to trap some important people of the enemy kingdom. Because the deployment of an army is expensive, one should try to minimise the role of the army and make use of the internal weaknesses of the enemy kingdom when the vijigishu wants to attack it.

Book X deals with military encampments, battlefields and battle engagements. Book XIII deals with how to capture the capital with the help of propaganda. Kautilya gives considerable importance to the role of propaganda in warfare. By propaganda, he means all kinds of false information. The vijigishu has to fabricate information to confuse the enemy, he should inflate his power through rumours. Kautilya explains the use of magic at many places, and how through magic the vijigishu can impact public opinion. He could also do it by proclaiming his association with the gods. Making active use of religion, magic, espionage and propaganda is considered an essential part of warfare.

In comparison to The Prince

The main similarity between Machiavelli's Prince and Kautilya's Arthasastra is that both the authors are interested in advising the king on how to maintain power and how to expand the kingdom. Comparisons are sometimes made in terms of how far these two authors believed in morality. Both of them indeed wanted, we can say, the kings to be moral. The king should have a character. But they believed that character in a traditional sense is not adequate or suitable for a king. The king should employ many strategies, tactics, many kinds of duplicities and lies to be able to handle the enemy, within or outside.

Kautilya said that the king's welfare is people's welfare, the king's happiness is people's happiness or the king should maintain dharma in his kingdom. But he said so not for the sake of the people, and only for the sake of retaining power. When Kautilya advises the king to invade some country, it is not to establish dharma there or to make the people happy there, but to expand the king's power.

The king is not seeking power to maintain dharma, he is not seeking power to make people happy, but he is maintaining dharma or making people happy to keep his power secure. This position is similar to that of Machiavelli. To both Machiavelli and Kautilya, power is the goal and not morality. Nor did they ever say, if some other king can make your people happier, you give up power to him in the interests of the people.

Unlike Machiavelli though, Kautilya did not make any explicit statements on why the king should not follow dharma. It is because

Machiavelli was facing a very specific moral code given by Christianity, whereas Kautilya was facing Hinduism which was very broad. Kautilya could recommend all kinds of activities for the king saying that in the end, the king wants to establish dharma.

There is some methodological difference between the two authors. Unlike Machiavelli, Kautilya does not give any historical or contemporary examples to substantiate his theoretical proposals. Kautilya states everything in terms of general statements without using any specific references.

Foreign policy

To Kautilya a neighbouring kingdom is an actual enemy or a potential enemy. Enmity is usually determined by geographical position. Your enemy has a neighbour who may be his enemy. Kautilya says your enemy's enemy is your friend, enemy's friend is enemy, and a friend's friend is a friend.

Kautilya thinks of neighbouring states as well as their neighbours in terms of enemies and friends. The vijigishu looks around his territory within a particular range. In this circle, he has states which can be described as enemies or friends. This is what is called a mandala, meaning a circle of states. This model can be called loose bi-centric international system. But Kautilya's world was only that of South Asia, and not anything beyond.

There can be certain non-aligned states with kings who are neither friends nor enemies. These kings are of two types. One is madhyama, who is a mediatory king who occupies a territory close to both the ambitious one, the vijigishu, and his immediate enemy in front. He is capable of helping both because he is neutral, or he could be resisting both of them equally. Or a non-aligned state can be of another type, which is udasina. It is a state that is not in the vicinity but further away and is very powerful.

Kautilya says foreign policy depends upon the power equation. Kautilya proposes what is called a six-fold policy, sadhgunya. Vigraha (hostility) and yana (attack) are what a superior should follow vis-a-vis an inferior. Hostility is like a cold war, whereas an attack is an actual war.

There are three policies to follow when the king is inferior to another king. These are sandhi (accommodation), samasraya (protection) and dvaidhibhava (double policy). "Whoever is inferior to another shall seek sandhi with him." There are many ways of making a sandhi. Making your army available to a superior king when he requires it is one kind. Giving a tribute is another kind. Ceding territory is another.

But if you are inferior and the other is superior, it doesn't mean you will forever remain in that position. Power can change. At any point of time though, you are inferior to somebody and superior to somebody, or you could be just equal to somebody. With equals, Kautilya proposes Asana. Asana means, "Neither is my enemy strong enough to destroy my works nor am I strong enough to destroy his." Kautilya doesn't give much importance to relations with equal powers. He doesn't have the concept of balance of power which modern IR thinkers consider a source of stability[i]. He spends only one chapter on the equal relationship.

The inferior king also follows protection and double policy. Protection comes at great cost. The inferior one may have to take permission to install an heir apparent. He should renounce independent foreign policy. Double policy means the inferior king acts on behalf of the superior king to harass the superior king's enemy.

Kautilya also proposes what are called upayas, which are sama, bheda, dana and danda – conciliation, dissension, gift and punishment. When a neighbouring king is only pretending friendship but is planning to attack you, according to what your espionage network tells you, then you can invite that king for a festival or a wedding or an elephant hunt, Kautilya says, to capture him and kill him. This is danda. If there are other ways of winning him through conciliation (sama) or gifting (dana), you can consider them. Dissension (bheda) is about creating division and confusion in the enemy.

Role of norms

Can a conquering king have no norms in his pursuit of power? A conquering king cannot do whatever he wants even if he has a lot of power. Kautilya's mandala model suggests that even if you are a great king, you would have many enemies. You are a part of a circle of states where you have friends as well as enemies.

If you do things that your friends wouldn't approve of, then you are increasing the risk of losing them. You can't do something to a state which could antagonise your friends. You will have more enemies then, which is not in your interests. There is something like an international society, where a king is subjected to certain norms.

There are limits to what the vijigishu can do to the neighbouring kingdoms. The conqueror does ashvamedha, a yagna, and releases a horse. If it goes unhindered in a kingdom it means that the kingdom has accepted the superiority of the conqueror. What then can the conqueror do? "The just vijigishu is satisfied with mere obeisance." The conqueror should not expect anything more than obeisance and certain things expected of an obedient state. The conqueror cannot seize the land or property of the defeated ruler. If he does, he would incur the hostility of the whole circle of states.

So conquering had a specific meaning in the context of ancient India, it didn't give the king the power to do anything. For example, the victorious king is not supposed to covet the wives of the defeated. Also, the circle of states will condemn the wealth acquired by breaching treaties and destroying friends. Conquering the world did not mean the emperor was a ruler with a tightly controlled administration over the entire territory, it simply meant many states would accept the superiority of the emperor. Anything more than that would mean more hostility, it would deprive the emperor of the support of the circle of the states. All this means there is some presence of international society with its moral code. The king had to consider it.

Think on it

1. Who is a vijigishu?
2. What is the role of espionage and propaganda in warfare?
3. What are the similarities between Machiavelli and Kautilya?
4. What are the differences between Machiavelli and Kautilya?
5. What is Kautilya's mandala theory?
6. How big was Kautilya's world?
7. How is Kautilya's world bi-centric?
8. How does Kautilya's foreign policy come under realism?
9. What can a conqueror do to the conquered kingdom?
10. Are there limits placed by the world on what a powerful king can do?

[i] Kautilya: Foreign Policy and International System in the Ancient Hindu World by George Modelski, JSTOR was helpful in understanding Kautilya' foreign policy.

The Buddha

What Would a Buddhist Offer to Political Thought?

How might a Buddhist react when he reads a standard textbook of political thought? Can his insight on nirvana help him to contribute anything to political thought? I think indeed there is a lot he can contribute.

Any political system aims to ensure the happiness of the people. A political system has various arrangements in place by which the people can lead happier lives. Political thought focuses on the role of the state in creating a happy society. How did the Western liberal democracies attempt to bring about happiness for the people? What are their assumptions? Could a Buddhist have any objections to this?

A Western liberal democracy assumes that every individual has certain desires. It is assumed that if these desires are satisfied, then a person is happy. The political system takes the desires as given and valid, and it assumes that a person is happy to the extent these desires are realised. And people also get into conflict with others in the pursuit of their desires. To handle the conflict, there is a law. To enforce this law, there is a state.

The quality, validity or satiability of individuals' desires are not judged. The desires are wrong only to the extent they may come into conflict with others' desires. It is said that your rights have limits only when they impinge on others' rights. This is the general model that is assumed.

(2) The Western models have a legislature, executive and judiciary. Each one of these seeks to be as powerful as possible, but the power of one is to be checked by the other. This arrangement is called checks and balances. What is assumed of individuals is also assumed of institutions. The pursuit of one's desires is checked by that of others. How the checks and balances work is spelt out in the constitution.

(3) This constitution has to be approved by the people. This is what is meant by popular sovereignty. It is the people who finally judge by what principles they want to live. The values that people come to hold are the values that guide the constitution. This is the essential arrangement of liberal democracy.

Buddhist perspective

Let's look at how a Buddhist might look at these assumptions and arrangements.

1. He would say maximising one's desires doesn't contribute to one's happiness. It's not that one should not try to realise one's desires, but that should not be one's main goal.
2. A Buddhist would say one has to look within and pursue inner happiness. It does not mean you don't try to change the external situation. You may try to change it and you may succeed in changing it. But you should understand that the primary source of happiness exists within you.
3. Don't think that a Buddhist would say that unless your ego is dissolved and you reach a stage of desirelessness, you will not be happy. You will become happier as you understand more of your true nature.

If the political system aims to make the people happy, a Buddhist would say, try to help people pursue this inner happiness. And that would require a suitable milieu. The enlightenment, the ultimate stage of happiness, is supposed to be facilitated by following the eight-fold path. Though it doesn't automatically lead to nirvana, it helps. The state should create a right environment for the people to help them pursue this eight-fold path.

A Buddhist would prefer a state that would promote the values of kindness, love, control over passions, nonviolence and so on among its people. If you have a conflict with another person, try to change that person nonviolently. If somebody wrongs you, do not hurt as a way of punishing, but try to change that person. The satyagraha approach that Gandhi followed is something a Buddhist state would encourage.

How do you resolve the conflict between countries? A Buddhist would say, don't promote hatred, and let not a nation take its identity and ego too seriously. Don't always think in terms of how your country is good and other countries are bad. This is what Tagore advocated in terms of internationalism. It is a Buddhist approach.

You are not going to be happier just by satisfying your desires more. Buddha advocated the satisfaction of minimum needs. One should lead a life of simplicity. A Buddhist state would encourage simple living that is meditative and self-reflective. It would discourage the accumulation of wealth and refuse to take wealth as a measure of man's worth. Such a state would be in a better position to satisfy the needs of all. Again, this is just what Gandhi too proposed.

On constitution

People frame the constitution of their country based on their assumptions about what makes them happy. But Buddha didn't think people know what makes them truly happy. Would Buddha create a democratic system? Any state based on certain religious ideas has this problem. But we can discuss from the point of view of Buddhist philosophy how Buddha would have tried to avoid this problem.

Firstly, Buddha did not say that you should follow him blindly. That was not his approach. Buddha said, this is the truth but you should try to understand it yourself and not simply take it from me. Buddha did not force anyone. Nor did he say anything like 'God told me and so you should listen'. What would Buddha have said about the constitution of liberal democracy? Maybe he would have said, 'Yes, that's a decent arrangement, to begin with.' But happiness calls for something else which we have to try to find out.

Ashoka

As to how a Buddhist would rule, we have an example from history, and that is Ashoka. We can't say Ashoka followed all the implications of Buddhist thought. He did certain things which were Buddhist. What was Ashoka's attitude towards various religions and sects as well as sects within Buddhism? Ashoka did not impose the Buddhist doctrine on the people. Tolerance would be a policy of the political system based on Buddhist teachings.

Can a Buddhist do away with the use of violence? Ashoka used force but, he said, only where necessary. A rock edict says that conquest by dhamma is preferable to Ashoka than conquest by force. Ashoka believed in convincing and transforming the people, and not in punishing, though he was willing to punish if needed.

What kind of foreign policy did Ashoka have? He was spreading dhamma to various countries, he sent his messengers. Ashoka was trying to create a world where people pursued dhamma or Buddhist religion.

In a Buddhist state, there should be an establishment of law and order, there should be trade, there should be agriculture, and there should be industry. It is just that in addition to these the state would also create the right conditions for people to pursue their inner happiness. People would not worship wealth and power alone.

Think on it

1. How would a Buddhist look at human desires?
2. What is the link between the people and their constitution in a democracy?
3. According to a Buddhist, what makes a person happy?
4. How would a Buddhist state focus on the needs of the people?
5. How would a Buddhist state relate itself to other states?
6. What was Ashoka's policy towards various religions?
7. How did Ashoka try to spread dhamma?
8. In what essential ways might a Buddhist state be different from liberal democracy?

CHAPTER THIRTY-THREE

Impact of Buddhist Traditions

It would be difficult to identify the impact of Buddhism per se on ancient Indian political thought because Hinduism and Buddhism are inseparable and both of them impacted ancient Indian political thought. Both religions share many fundamental concepts: the idea of dharma, karma, soul, and rebirth though with somewhat different explanations. Even a scripture that is considered central to Hinduism, the Bhagavad Gita, was impacted by Buddhism[1].

One clear difference between Buddhism and Hinduism is Buddhism's egalitarian outlook. Buddhism didn't believe that a king had any divine right to rule. Buddhist thought takes the state as a kind of social contract. On the other hand, Hinduism holds the preservation of the caste system to be an important aspect of Dharma. It also gives importance to Brahmin supremacy, rituals and sacrifices.

Impact of Ashoka

To the extent Ashoka impacted political thought, we can consider it the impact of Buddhist traditions on political thought. Ashoka was a committed Buddhist and he wanted the state to propagate Buddhism and inculcate Dharma in people. Ashoka believed in conquest by Dharma rather than conquest by force, within his kingdom and outside. He sent many missions to propagate Buddhism in Sri Lanka, Europe and even Africa. Buddhism to him meant treating his people as his children and working for them, which led to the welfare orientation of the state. This is what Ashoka's rock edicts[2] said:

"Thereafter, now, the Kalingas annexed, became intense His Sacred Majesty's observance of Dharma, love of Dharma, and his preaching of the Dharma, moral conquest is considered the principal conquest" (Rock Edict, XIII). Kalinga was the last war waged by Ashoka.

"Known is it to you.. to what extent is my reverence as well as faith in the Buddha, the Dharma and the Samgha. Whatsoever has been said by the Lord Buddha, all that has of course been well said" (Rock Edict, II). Ashoka accepted Buddhism in toto.

"Now ceremonies should certainly be performed. But these bear little fruit. That, however, is productive of great fruit which is connected with Dharma" (Rock Edict, IX).

"All men are my children. As, on behalf of my own children, I desire that they may be provided with complete welfare and happiness both in this world and the next" (Rock Edict I). Welfare was the goal.

"At all hours, when I am eating, or in the harem, or the place or religious instructions, or the parks, everywhere, Prativedakas (overseers) are posted with instructions to report on the affairs of the people. In all places do I dispose of the affairs of the people" (Rock Edict, VI). This one says how accessible Ashoka wanted to be to the people.

Ashoka was tolerant of other religions. "In all places should reside people of diverse sects. For they all desire restraint of passions and purity of heart. But men are of various inclinations and various passions. They may thus perform the whole or a part of their duties" (Rock Edict, XII).

Ashoka believed that the purpose of the state is to promote morality. "The Rajukas (provincial governors) shall acquaint themselves with what causes happiness and misery, and, with the help of the pious, admonish the people of the provinces that they may gain both here and hereafter" (RE IV). This is like its modern equivalent of the administration trying to introduce behavioural change. Ashoka even went for setting up the institution of Dharma-Mahamastras. "They have been employed among all the sects for the establishment and growth of Dharma and the good and happiness of those devoted to religion" (Rock Edict, V).

The purpose of the state is to promote dharma. Hinduism also believed that a king should follow dharma and should promote dharma, but no Hindu king did it with the conviction that Ashoka did it.

Buddhism didn't believe in the divine right rule of the king. But it didn't matter to Ashoka. He was both the head of religion and the head of the state. Previously, the Brahmins were the interpreters of Dharma and the king was supposed to follow it. During Ashoka's regime, Ashoka himself became the interpreter of the religion. He was not being dictated by anyone.

How was Ashoka different from the king that Kautilya wanted? To Kautilya, the king should follow Dharma, but only to strengthen politics. Ashoka was interested in Dharma for its own sake. But his pursuit of Dharma strengthened him and he became a great king. As a part of his Dharma, he worked for the welfare of the people. All that contributed to a strong polity, which Kautilya also wanted. Overall, Ashoka raised the standards by which any future king of India would be judged.

Think on it

1. What are the concepts common to Hinduism and Buddhism?
2. Where does Buddhism differ from Hinduism?
3. What was Ashoka's attitude towards other faiths?
4. What was the purpose of Ashoka's state?
5. What is Ashoka's contribution to political thought?

[1] This is discussed elaborately in my book Caste and Religion in India.

[2] I took the edicts and some of the points from The Place of Emperor Asoka in Ancient Indian Political Thought by Henry Albinski, available at JSTOR.

Ramana Maharshi

CHAPTER THIRTY-FOUR

Hinduism as Eternal and Realisable Truth

Why are we discussing religion while doing political thought? Religion is important because in India people only had an identity of religion for centuries, Hindus and Muslims, or caste. There was nothing like being an Indian. Reformers in the modern period were trying to find what it is to be a Hindu or to be a Muslim. They were trying to figure out their past and shape their future as members of a particular religion. In that way, the issue of religion comes up again and again in Indian political thought.

In Hinduism, many people have tried to reform and refine the religion, saying that this is Hinduism and this is not Hinduism, and these are the evils of Hinduism, this is how to change them while still being a Hindu. They quoted scriptures in their support.

Usually, when a historian wants to study Hinduism, he may want to study the scriptures. There are Vedas and Upanishads, or the Gita. I believe there can also be a different approach. We can learn about Hinduism by examining what is happening to the people who are seen as the highest expressions of the religion.

Most people would agree that Ramana Maharshi (1879–1950) represented the highest and the purest manifestation of Hinduism. By examining what he taught in a very simple language, maybe we can try to understand the experience that is exalted in Hinduism, that of moksha. Interestingly, Ramana Maharshi not only explained what he experienced, but he also produced some enlightened disciples. One of them was H. W. L. Poonja (1910–97), who was called Papaji and was from Lucknow. He produced another enlightened disciple, Mooji (b. 1954), who is a Jamaican now living in Portugal. He is now teaching the essence of the wisdom of Ramana Maharshi and Papaji, perhaps in a more elaborate form.

If you ask me where is the highest aspect of Hinduism being expressed in its purest form currently, I will say it is in Portugal and by Mooji. There is one more person, Ekhart Tolle (b. 1948) who is a German. He had an experience of enlightenment on his own, and then he read Hindu and Buddhist traditions to explain and consolidate his own experience. You can also learn from Eckhart Tolle what Hinduism is essentially about.

Explaining moksha

Let me explain this fundamental transformation called moksha using minimum number of terms, namely, memory, mind, ego and self. Memory is our past stored in the brain. Some of the memories are charged plus or minus, pleasant or unpleasant. A part of the total memory deals with our notion of ourselves, forming ideas like 'I am this', 'I am going to be this', 'I got hurt', 'I was happy', 'This is what I like', or 'I don't like this'. Let's call it the ego.

What is the mind? A big part of the mind is ego thinking in terms of 'What am I going to be?' as in 'I am going to be an IAS topper', 'I am going to prove my worth', 'I will be a politician'. The mind thinks and thinks a lot. All this thinking about oneself is the mind. There is also thinking unrelated to the ego which is part of the mind but is not related to the transformation we are discussing.

The physical infrastructure for the mind as well as the memory is the brain. The brain is the physical thing, the brain can be touched, but the mind cannot be touched. The brain is hardware, the mind is like software.

Normally, we equate ourselves with our minds. To the question 'Who am I', we answer, this is my past, this is my present, this is my future, this is what I like, this is what I want to do and so on. The 'me' is my mind. This is a common understanding.

Ramana Maharshi would say, "If you are saying 'this is my mind', then you are not your mind. For the mind to be yours, you have to be other than the mind." Ramana says, "You are not your mind." Ramana exhorts the seeker to ask 'Who am I?' Who is observing the mind and owning the mind? Ramana says that which is observing is the real you. It can be called self. Self is simply awareness or consciousness. The consciousness is observing the mind, it is not the mind. You are not your mind, you are pure consciousness.

Consciousness and self are all the same. Ramana tells you to consider the self as you, not your mind. Let it observe the mind. The ego generates thoughts. Just observe. Observe the thoughts as an outsider because you are indeed an outsider, you are not your mind. Let the mind have its thoughts. Let them be good or bad, you don't bother. Just watch them like you watch a movie. Get out of the idea that you are the mind and realise that you are the awareness.

Where is the self located? There is something that science has discovered only recently. According to Antonio Damasio, a neuroscientist, the self (or consciousness) emerged as a result of evolution. It is there only in higher life forms and it is located in the brainstem. Damage to a particular spot in the brainstem can make a person lose the sense of self. It can take him to a coma. We also lose the sense of self during deep sleep. During dreams, we lose it partially.

When we observe the mind from the vantage of the self, then the mind loses its importance hugely, and the ego shrinks and surfaces sporadically. It is not that the ego disappears altogether. It only becomes less significant.

The ego has a function. It selects memory, it defines what one is good at. It defines your comfort zone. It recognises dangers and can instantly react. The ego persists but has shrunk, it doesn't produce so much of mind.

A realised person is not with his mind the whole time like normal people are. The mind simply comes and goes as he wants it. He can use the mind when he wants to use it. A realised person can experience vast stretches of no mind, complete silence, and complete calmness.

Ordinarily, those who want to introspect themselves split the mind into parts. One part of the mind will be observing another part. The part of the mind wanting to work hard condemns that which is lazy. There is a conflict between the fragments of the mind – the ego identifying itself with one part and trying to manage the other part. Ramana says just don't that, don't try to reform the mind, simply disown it. Let the mind do whatever it wants to do, don't try to be good, don't avoid bad, and let the whole enterprise of the mind lose its importance.

This freedom from the mind is considered real freedom, it is not freedom from any external authority or internally set goals. Otherwise, you are enslaved by your mind. This seems to be the essence of moksha. Ramana lived this, and so did Papaji.

There is an interesting parallel between Papaji and Ramakrishna Paramahamsa. Papaji also used to see gods, particularly he used to see Krishna, and he used to play with him.

Ramana Maharshi once asked Papaji 'What are you doing?'

Papaji said, 'I was playing with Krishna.'

'Really? You like him?'

'Yes, I like him.'

'Where is he now?'

'He is not with me now.'

'Whatever comes and goes is not permanent. Find out what is permanent.'

Papaji understood what is permanent is self and dropped Krishna. Had Ramakrishna Paramahamsa met someone like Ramana Maharshi, he might have changed.

As a young man, Eckhart Tolle was hugely depressed. He wanted to kill himself. He did not like himself. One night he thought, 'I am not liking myself, but what is me, what is it that does not like me?'

He was puzzled. Then he found that he is the self, and not the mind. He became calm.

This process of self-enquiry leading to enormous silence and quietude seems to be the transformation the yogis of this land dreamt of, all through the ages. Why is this also considered freedom from sorrow? Because you will take your mind and its agonies as you currently take others' minds and their agonies – and not more than that. The way you watch a movie, you watch your mind – the movie could sometimes be a tragedy.

This, I would say, is the essence of Hinduism, but this also appears to be the basis for mystical experiences across religions, whether is Sufism or Christian mysticism.

Think on it

1. What do you know about Ramana Maharshi?
2. Who is Papaji?
3. Who is Mooji?
4. Who is Echart Tolle?
5. What is ego?
6. What is the self?
7. Is the self the same as consciousness?
8. How is the ego related to the mind?
9. Where is self located in the body?
10. What is common to coma and deep sleep?
11. What is the role of the ego in generating thought?
12. What is supposed to be the right relationship between the self and the mind?
13. What is expected to happen to the ego and the mind as they are put under observation?
14. Will the ego ever completely disappear?
15. What is freedom from sorrow?

Sources

1. Political Thought in Modern India edited by Thomas Pantham, Kenneth L Deutsch (1986)

2. Modern Indian Political Thought: Text and Context by Bidyut Chakravarty and Rajendra Kumar Pandey (2009)

3. Foundations of Indian Political Thought by V.R.Mehta (1996)

4. Indian Political Thought: Themes and Thinkers by Himanshu Roy and M.P.Singh (2017)

5. Tagore & Gandhi: Walking Alone and Walking Together by Rudrangshu Mukherjee (2021)

6. Makers of Modern India edited and introduced by Ramachandra Guha (2010)

7. Pakistan Or The Partition of India by B.R.Ambedkar (1945)

8. Savarkar and Hindutva: The Godse Connection by A.G.Noorani (2002)

9. The Great Speeches of Modern India edited by Rudrangsu Mukherjee

8. Articles from JSTOR, Wikipedia

9 798888 722917